Cleuber Cristiano de Sousa

Psychoanalytical psychopathology

AF209953

Cleuber Cristiano de Sousa

Psychoanalytical psychopathology

The study of man by the determination of his desires and unconscious conflicts

ScienciaScripts

This book is a translation from the original published under ISBN 978-620-0-80294-1.

Publisher:
Sciencia Scripts
is a trademark of
International Book Market Service Ltd., member of OmniScriptum Publishing Group
17 Meldrum Street, Beau Bassin 71504, Mauritius
Printed at: see last page
ISBN: 978-620-0-92077-5

PSYCHOANALYTICAL PATHOLOGY

The study of man by the determination of his unconscious desires and conflicts.

Cleuber Cristiano de Sousa

Psychoanalyst

Psychopathologist

Index

PRESENTATION

Psychoanalysis is inserted in this 21st century in a scenario totally fertile by the diversity of identification and by the ways of resonance and multiple relations of collectivity, both with regard to the dynamic phenomena of globalization by the pandemic and the current dissonants and proposals for the constitution of subjects, history, symbolic and an imaginary that has rescued memorable from a restored concatenation of the primal order.

This study also has the function of making possible a proposal that reaches the observation, diagnosis and intervention and primary care of the subject who is subjective. In this orientation, it is the work of the analyst to understand the constitutive process of the semiology of disorders and other psychopathological signs and symptoms and, also, how this whole organized set is physiologically perceived. The contribution of this research is in the psychopathological action related to the foundations of dynamic, descriptive, existential, sociocultural, biological, operational-pragmatic, medical, categorical, behavioral, dimensional, fundamental, and psychoanalytical analysis, and, in the light of nosology, nosography and their respective objects of study, to erupt the subject touched by the symbolic and pinched by history.

However, it is in etiopathogeny that the diagnosis of an explanatory nature is based. In Nosography, what is presented is a written exposition, a description of the diseases, with specific orientation to the precise diagnosis and intervention/interventions for an effective treatment, but it is in the social relations that the experiences give form and outline to the symptomatic object.

Alterations, whether due to a similar chronology or to development, are the most frequent complaints regarding signs, symptoms, disorders and neurodevelopment disorders. This clinical reality is a worrying factor for the various segments that articulate themselves in the referential of normality in development and, later, the manifestations by comorbidity of other signs and symptoms.

It is known that clinically the physiological alterations are not limited to the biological aspects of neurodevelopment, but it is from these limits that we will initially manifest our fundamental considerations on the relationship of the psychoanalysis/psychopathology binomial. But this develops and evolves in large steps to a reverberant motility of psychoanalytic psychopathology.

According to Gabbard (1984), the formulations of the objective relationships derived from clinical observations were sustained and elaborated by the studies of baby observations conducted by Margaret Mahler. She and her collaborators identified three phases: autistic phase (2 first months of life), symbiosis (between 2 and 6 months) and separation-individuation (four subphases) - differentiation (6 and 10 months), practice (10 and 16 months), rapprochement (16 and 24 months) and consolidation of individuality (third year of life).

Just like magnetic resonance imaging is the most clinician-oriented examination that captures high-resolution images of tissues and organs of the human body/organism, with increasingly modern and practical diagnostic methods, being a powerful and versatile non-invasive examination, nosographic and nosological psychopathology is a fundamental instrument for the investigative monitoring of the entire anatomophysiological apparatus of man. None of this reveals its essence. There is no exam capable of bringing out what is formless. And our subjective nature is shapeless. In order to be the welcome and welcome guest, we must be the messengers of dissociations and, in order to do so, repeatedly assume the imaginative materiality of their resonance.

SCHOOLS OF THOUGHT

EGO SCHOOL

According to the German psychologist Kurt Lewin, *if you really want to understand something it is necessary that you try to modify what you want to* understand, contributing with your experiences and interventions in the environment in which you live and making available efforts for self-analysis and self-knowledge with the objective of mobilizing methodologies for the reproduction of assertiveness methods. But the greatest contribution of Lewin's theories, regarding his studies of social psychology, was in the famous quote: *"Nothing is as practical as a good theory".* This affirmation makes it possible to raise how much the knowledge and recognition of psychoanalytic theory, the seven schools, their thinkers and the objects studied, as well as the curves and insertions, must be apprehended with acuity for the maintenance of the integrity of the object of study, which after its understanding, can and must be analyzed by an updated lens that reaches the evolution of the subject, its history, its symbolic and how this must be articulated in a clinic of the imperfect. The legacy of psychoanalytical theory is fundamental for other areas, such as dynamic psychiatry, and a precise articulation between theory, method and practice/analysis is necessary for the assertive action of the professionals who are involved in this clinic. The theory in analysis is what guides the analyst in deciding what to say, when to say it, for whom to say it and what would be more prudent not to say, at least in that *analytical setting (therapeutic alliance).* Thus, we have three schools that are theoretical milestones of Dynamic Psychiatry: The Psychology of the Ego, with essays and bases sediment in the classical study of Freudian psychoanalytic theory, from the 1st clinic, with all its assumptions: Transference, Oedipus Complex, Sexuality Theory and Metapsychology (Topics I and II). Besides this theoretical contribution, H. Kohut's Psychology of the Self, revisited by him on the basis of Harry Stack Sullivan, who studied the relatively long-lasting pattern of interpersonal relationships that characterize a human life. And the other foundation school is called the Theory of Object Relations, by Melanie Klein and Winnicott. It is from these schools of thought that the performance in situations of analysis and intervention will be presented.

We will then start with the Psychology of Ego, which has its object the topographic model: Topic 1 and Topic 2 - Unconscious, Pre-conscious and Conscious/Id, Ego and Superego. The traumatic content that was repressed of the disgusting experiences was propelling symptoms that the hysterical "de Freud" presented in their session reports. The memories that were hidden by the traumas and repressed were converted into somatological symptoms. For Freud, there would be the action of Psychoanalysis as a therapy of suspension of the element of recalculation, of the traumatic, painful and impacting events that were subdued and filed. This mechanism of defense of the ego is the origin of Freudian researches and the most important under the aegis of neurosis. Freud in 1895 wrote the "Project" (Project for a Scientific Psychology, 1893-1895) and between 1923-1925, The Ego and Id and other works. The function of the recalcitrant defense mechanism is to erase from the unconscious the bias of the most profound and impacting affective and relational experiences in the life of the constituted subject. For Freud, the analysis was the method by which the recalculation would be suspended and the stressful experiential experiences would come to the surface, would emerge as remembered memories and would, from then on, be possible to be treated and suffer action by the analyst. It is in the manifestation of the traumatic event remembered by the free association, in speech, that the symptom should be treated through the empathy of the analyst in question. "Like a young girl for having a paralyzed arm, because in a daydream she has the idea of her father being *stung* by a snake, but not reaching it, for having his arm asleep by the back of the chair. And only after remembering this event." It is thus in free association that it is possible to "clean the chimney" and in the expression of the repressed feeling that the repressing would be suspended by the cathartic method. By making the traumatic memory unconscious, that is, the stressful events have, in this way, the liberation of the recalculated psychic energy. When Freud realized that the analyzer was resisting to his psychic *interactions*, he felt the need to review the methodology used in the topic and to know why traumatic memories could not emerge. The defense mechanisms that forced the failure in the topographic model were unconscious, which led Freud to identify unconscious formations in the ego, besides the conscious ones.

The theory called the tripartite structure of topic 2 would then bring the id, ego and superego, cut by id and constituted by desire. The Psychology of the Ego is responsible for the definition of the intrapsychic universe in what we refer to the narrow conflicts: id, ego and superego. For Psychodynamic Psychiatry, the superego, the ego and the id maintain a battle among themselves, while expression and discharge are the way in which the demands of sexuality and aggressiveness are received. According to Freud (1926/1959), anxiety is the result of the conflict between the instances, that is, it is a product of him. "This signaling anxiety alerts the ego of the need for a defense mechanism" (FREUD. S., 1926/1959). It is through this process that one can understand the formation of the neurotic symptom in psychoanalytic theory. Based on the above process, the symptom would be a commitment foma, which is a mechanism of defense of the imperious imposition of the ID/desire, but gratifies it in an attenuated and masked way.

EGO MECHANISMS

Rationalization: When socially deformed and considered unacceptable behaviors are justified by rationalism, logic or operational scientificity.

"I wear a headset at work so I don't listen to my colleagues' parallel conversations. This gets in my way!"

Reactive training: Using diametrically opposed behaviors (opposition) to prevent or attenuate the expression or verbalization of inappropriate thoughts or feelings (without acceptability).

"The mayor has a farm and does not respect the orientation towards space without deforestation, according to the orientation towards sustainable environment and during an environmental assembly, he says: there is no sustainability and preservation with deforestation!

Isolation: dissociating the remembrance or thought from the feeling or emotion related to the event remembered.

"A daughter describes the brutal murder of her mother, whom she loved so much, without expressing any emotion."

Compensation: A distorted relationship of covering up undesirable behavior or weakness for another socially accepted.

"A son who's not good at sports becomes studious and very dedicated."

Displacement: the transfer of a feeling to another that you consider less harmful or threatening.

"Instead of responding directly to the parents, the teenager verbally assaults the sister."

Denial: the intentional refusal of the appearance of a situation or the affective or sentimental relationships linked to the event.

"Subject smokes more than one cigarette wallet a day, but naturalizes the suit."

Regression: returning to the previous phases, with the same or similar behaviors of comfort, for a situation that generates fear or anxiety.

"When she divorces, Ana goes back to sleep hugging the teddy bear."

Identification: the use of characteristics that you admire to overcome your own difficulties or weaknesses.

"After seeing a shark attack on an individual and the rescue by a surfer, John decides to learn how to surf."

*Repression: Excluding from consciousness feelings or affections that have become unpleasant or traumatic, in an involuntary manner.

"A victim of physical aggression and death threat can't remember anything after being assaulted."

Intellectualization: the use of logic and reason to cover up unpleasant feelings or sensations.

"Your son's move abroad being justified by the opportunity to work successfully."

Sublimation: Reordering or redirecting to socially constructive and desirable impulses of socially unacceptable actions or attitudes.

"A smoker who becomes the leader of an anti-smoking NGO."

Introjection: integration to the ego of other subjects' values.

"Integrate habits or behaviors (thoughts and values) of the new inhabitants/neighbors of the community to which you recently belong."

Suppression: the voluntary retention of unpleasant or traumatic feelings.

"After not being approved in the selection for the job she had so dreamed of, Maria decided not to remember it now."

Annulment: Annul an unpleasant feeling for a symbolically attractive or socially desirable one.

"The clerk arrived late and brought the candy his boss likes so much and a chocolate that brings him well-being."

SCHOOL OF OBJECTIVE RELATIONS THEORY

The thought of the Psychology of the Ego that objective relationships are secondary in relation to the first impulse (thus attributing a privileged *locus* to aggressiveness and sexuality). The accepted mechanism is the discharge of tension, being under the pressure of the pulsions. In a different orientation, the ORT sees the mother-baby diode as a good example of the relationship being a propeller of impulses, which can be positive or not.

The impulses are primarily linked to the search for the object, rather than voltage reduction. (Gabbard apud Fairbain. p. 44: 1994).

When interpersonal relationships are transformed into internalized representations of relationships, we can say that the foundation of the theory of objective relationships is present. As Ferbain (1940) recommends, the child's development allows him/her to internalize not only a person or object, but as he/she widens his/her life path, the internalization is also extended to complete relationships. Freud (1905) said that an example of a positive love experience is the baby's nursing period. The relationships between the positive experience of the self (baby) and that of the object (loving mother) is a positive affective experience. The pleasure and satisfaction of self-conservation and survival consolidates this model. The negative experience can come later when hunger comes and the mother is not available for the act, producing then a negative experience of the self (desirous and frustrated), with a careless and indifferent object, and a negative experience of anger. These representations coexist between pleasure and horror, internalized in two distinct groups of objective relationships. The maternal physical sensations during breastfeeding and their presence during the act are initial elements that give rise to introjection. According to Schafer (1968), this is the usual reference to the internalization of the mother. This has its mark from the sixteenth month of life, when there is a limit between the internal and external in this individuation. The development of the cognitive apparatus, that is, perception is the mechanism that makes the transformation between the representation of the object (what is good) that originates hallucinatory desire in an internal presence. The terror of the latent of losing the mother is an insistent propeller of the positive and loving feelings of the mother. Understanding the reasons for introjection (penetration) of "good" positive feelings seems to be more accessible, since the bad/negative ones lack factors or aspects that are well elucidated for description. An example that seems very likely to me is that a mother unwilling to gratify her child may be related only to another doing and not necessarily to a disintegrating allusion of positive feelings directed to the baby, but is experienced, experienced and more, introjected, as aggressive, rejecting, violent, hostile and without affable availability by the infant. In this other orientation by the theory of objective relations, there is a prominent inaccuracy between the real object and the internalized representation of this object. In internal objective relations, representations of the self, representations of objects and affections degrade to reverberate their voices in an intrapsychic scene. In the suborganizations, we can signal the importance of the Freudian concept, admitted in this composition as a foreign body.

Klein (1946) already signaled the primary terror of death *instinct* annihilation experienced by the baby in the first months of life. It is in *splitting* that the projection of aggressiveness derived from the death drive for the mother is oriented. The schizoparanoid position is the constitutive fear of the result of this projection, which allows after the dissociation of the ego, the fear that the mother will annihilate the libido that was formed inside the child. The term schizoid is justified by the dissociation of the ego and paranoid by the projection.

Important Considerations of the Theory of Objective Relations

1.   Privileged position of the self, in its objective relations in the psychic apparatus.

2.   Relationship with the tripartite formulation of *ich*'s impersonality.

3.   For Hartmann (1950), there is a distinction between ego and self, the reference for uses being the context of the interaction of objects. While the ego interacts with the id and the superego, the objects are the interaction of the self.

4.   Meissner (1986) ratifies that the development of the self takes place as the final product of interactions with objects of significance in the environment and with their corresponding internal objects.

5.   Neurotic defense mechanisms:

a.   Dissociation: Unconscious process that dynamically distinguishes feelings, representations of the self, or contradictory objective representations.

b.   Projective Identification: Stages of renegation of aspects of the individual and assignment to another person.

c.   Introjection: external object is symbolically introduced, taken and assimilated as part of the individual.

d.   Denial: Direct rejection of traumatic sensory data.

SELF SCHOOL

According to the Psychology of the Self, external relationships contribute to the maintenance of self-knowledge, self-analysis and self-esteem and, in this orientation, concatine the elements of cohesion of the self. The basis of this school of thought approach is based on the assertion of responsiveness on the part of other people in social life so that their well-being and self-esteem are in coherence and cohesion. Being well with yourself relates to the world being well with them. This theoretical current comes from the studies of Heinz Kohut (1971) and has a certain relationship with bipersonal psychology (Jaenick, 1987). It can be affirmed that the Psychology of the Self is the result of outpatient studies with patients with narcissistic disorders and that psychoanalytical psychotherapy is used for the treatment in question. In these studies, a pragmatic distinction was observed between these narcissistic patients and others who presented compulsive or even hysterical symptoms and their common symptomatic manifestations. Kohut (1971) concluded that there was a complaint of sudden and unusual feelings in what was related to classic symptoms of depression or wear and tear in relationships of all kinds. In these situations, they showed an apparent fragility to other people's considerations and the individual remained apathetic in the face of criticism from the community to which he belongs, becoming increasingly dissatisfied. In this way, treating this vulnerability of self-esteem and sensitivity to the external component by the Psychology of the Ego model would be ineffective and would contribute to clinical labor failure. It is in the study of transfers called specular, which refers to validation by the analyst, and in the idealizer, rescuing affection and parental care and protection, that Kohut starts to understand the symptoms and symptomatic manifestations of patients in this state. In the denomination of self grandiose exhibitionist, Kohut gave rise to the need for confirmation of the demonstrations of success and affirmation of conduct. Specular responses play an important role in the child's life in maintaining the child's self-assertion by the parents' affirmation. If this validation is not configured, the self disintegrates, giving the child the need to strive for an *optimum* result, by corroborating the ideological attainment of perfection. The unbridled search for this affirmation leads to an idealizing path of narcissistic compulsion in search of perfection. The representation of patients in search of validation and confirmation by the analyst refers to this puerile form of demonstration of child exhibitionism. The specular transference, then, besides demonstrating fragility, vulnerability and excessive sensitivity, orients towards a return to the affections of its primal history. Speculation and idealization are traces of previous phases that, for not being consolidated in successful psychic formations, provided the emergence of a brittle ego. This school of thought of Kohutian formulation strongly criticized the classical Freudian primacy that the initial narcissistic phase should be overcome for an objective transference as a presupposition of the natural process of maturation of the object of the self. For Kohut, the Freudian premises saw in the classical primary narcissistic model the transposition of a narcissistic reference being supplanted to make room for the demands of the external world and other people. In Kohut's thought this abandonment is if not unnecessary unattainable, being mobilized as energy for all life, even in situations of development of objective love of external transference or to an axis of external corporeality. Kohut's postulates followed the orientation of the dual-axis theory, which dealt with the parallelism between narcissism and objective love, not opposing the strategies of recurrence of capturing the broken maternal bond: grandiose self, of an internal ideological order of perfection constitutive of its satisfaction in itself, thus providing the ambitions and goals; and from the idealized parental image/image that is attributed to the parent its most genuine form of satisfaction and internalized, the ideas of the self emerge from there. The bipolar self for Kohut then refers to these two sources. Nevertheless, it would be presented by Kohut in his last work *How Heals Psychoanalysis?* (1984), an insertion in this concept for a tripolar self, having in this third pole what he called *alter ego* or gemelarity (something like gemelar self object, of generic constitution of being). This characteristic becomes efficient in the transference, moment in which the analyst feels invited to be like his analyst, thus making possible an area, in the meantime, of intermediate of other abilities and new talents, that touches the arc of tension between the poles of idealization and grandiosity. Diametrically in a different position to the classic psychoanalysis of the ego, which sees the infantile needs of parental mirroring as weakness, the psychology of the self corroborates the necessity of these specular and idealizing relations, as necessary to the natural mental organization. An important data for an updated research in psychoanalysis by the School of Self Psychology Thought is the need of the analyst to develop an empathy for the narcissistic needs of his analysands and in this way not to censure, restrain or cover up such demands. The Oedipus complex has no central relevance in the studies of Psychology of the Self. There is not a prominent condition for its relationship with the development of psychic formations, it is seen as a decomposer of the matrix failure of objects of the self. This attenuates the cuts of the superego in the formation of the subject's personality. The Oedipus complex of secondary valuation can be overcome by the matrix satisfaction of the objective needs of the infantile self before a symptom manifests itself. For the Psychology of the Self it is not the consequence of neurotic conflict by the anxiety of castration, but in the anxiety of disintegration, as a result of inadequate responses of the object of the self. Obsessive behavior disorders and sexual compulsions and perversions are a frustrated attempt to contain symptoms resulting from excesses of pulsional vicissitudes and degrading and exhausting for a restoration of the object of the self. The measurability of this fragmentation is relative, because it ranges from mild anxiety symptoms to panic, with somatological linkage by symptomatic conversion (from psychic to somatose). It is in the relevance of self-esteem for the evolution of psychopathological symptoms that Kohut's main contribution to Psychodynamic Psychiatry is presented. In the studies of the self of babies, we have in Daniel Stern (1985) the most prominent figure. He was the forerunner of the division between the appearance of one sense of self and the other in tune with the responses of the mother or caregivers. He also minimized the role of fantasy, in opposition to Klein's ideas, being his behaviour adherent to reality. Stern stated that history, coherence, affection, action were indispensable aspects for the constitution of the sense of self. This history has to do with the continuity of psychic and social processes.

The patient must be allowed to lead the clinician to any theoretical sphere that best suits the clinical material.

(Gabbard. p. 57: 1994)

According to Gabbard (1984), familiarity with all three theoretical models of dynamic psychiatry (Schools of Thought of Psychoanalysis: Ego, Self and TRO) requires a greater breadth of knowledge, but also allows a richer understanding of patients and their psychopathology.

It is always more efficient and cautious to use maps, compasses and other cartography and orienteering equipment when you launch yourself to reach a point in the middle of the unknown. The theoretical schools of psychoanalysis are these essential elements, which more than instruments of use and disuse, are mechanisms for understanding the dynamic functioning of the psychic apparatus. They are the safe north guided by the referencing of its objects of study. In the course, at the beginning of this journey, there are at least three in encounter with the imbrication of its purpose: the subject who sees himself (reading of himself), what one sees of this subject (reading of the other) and the subject as he constitutively is (the real of the subject).

SOCIAL ORIENTATION OF THE WORD - SCIENCE AND PSYCHOANALYSIS

In the communication process, part of the conceptual validation has to do with how an analysis develops and continues and to which theory it belongs. Knowledge of the difference between the conceptual framework and the theoretical framework is indispensable for a positioning before the paradigms of science. For that, in a qualitative instance of the research project, it is necessary to know the impact on social realities and its methodological scope.

It is worth saying that a proposal based on language materializes in the transformation of abstract assumptions into material instruments of cultural change in society. Knowing the contribution in the human, social, cultural field and how the contributive impulse in the various instances of science would be, is essential for the composition of an investigative project in any space of social change that involves language, subject and exteriority.

The scientific paradigm is embodied in the relational aspects of understanding the world, its social reality and the spectrum of the process in the constitution of the link between a given object of study and its respective researcher. This subject, from a constructivist perspective, is symbolically mediated by the social-historical aspects, in an ermic and ethical behavior, from the paradigmatic point of view. These processes are represented through their ontological, epistemological and methodological nature, in order to adjust themselves to a positivist, postpositivist (neopositivist) positioning of critical theory and constructivism, according to the object under analysis and the symbolic world of those involved.

For Guba (1990:17), the paradigm, or interpretative scheme, is a set of beliefs that guide action. Thus, when choosing a paradigm, the researcher selects his path by which he will adjust the clippings and phenomenological aspects of his research. These paths are multiple and not determined, because their nature is eminently social, challenged by language in its ideological sense.

Interpretative paradigms are characterized according to their epistemological, ontological and methodological nature in positivist, post-positivist, critical and constructivist-interpretative theory. Heterogeneity is the fundamental mark of all decentralized thinking. When thinking about science, in its methodological constitution, the rigor of methods, the systematic form and the requirements of scientific knowledge, a theoretical reorganization and a methodological shift are necessary to overcome a legalistic aspect, because the paths that lead to explain and predict are not only rhetorical.

The logical and empirical foundations are responsible for both coherence and empirical contrast, relating to temporal, factual and spatial aspects, yet in a world constituted by social representations there is no room for a reductionist rationalism or a behaviorist empiricism, when the theme is the language and constitution of the social subject.

Science is thus a social practice, that is, historical, because it is built in consonance with the transformations of society in a given time and space, in constant and non-linear movement, because this temporality is not chronological but conceived by memory. One cannot deny the importance of the demonstrative sciences for the construction of historicization and the composition of the investigative subject that we have in post-modern social sciences, but this model corresponds to a rationalist neutrality.

In this instance, the denial of the ideologically neutral is the hallmark of the recognition of increasingly broad and interconnected horizons of expectations in a coalition knowledge society. In the meantime, scientific is what can be explained, predicted, interpreted and understood. For modernity, the demonstrative sciences tried to explain and, thus, made the study logical and capable of being measured and apprehended, through an experimental, verifiable and manipulative methodology.

On the whole, it can be understood that the laws that govern nature are embodied in the assumption that knowledge should not be legalistic, thus dispensing with the interest of modern science to, at last, seek a slide that is affiliated to the social orientation of the word. Postmodern thinking no longer rests on pre-established truths, because it understands the complexity of relationships in all themes and approaches.

This complexity extends to the subjective role of the subject who builds his social reality outside of Cartesian and minimalist thinking. Thus, rationalist reasoning is not conceived, especially if the object is the subject's language, subjectivity and ideological constitution, which is historical and social and claims the irruption of multiple, polysemic and polyphonic meaning.

This dynamic is articulated, allowing the investigation mediated by values, with the intention of interpretation and understanding, and not only characterized by appreciable and measurable explanation. The object of study is a creation an effect, the basis that presents itself as a referential parameter for something to be investigated, from a defined point of view, but with a retina that recognizes the historical and social interfaces. It is necessary to identify these relations, since it is from this that the surrounding elements are observed that will be analyzed, aggregated, opposed or regulated and justified, respecting all the representative and material boundaries of the study.

The object of study then becomes the driving point of writing and the social orientation of the word. The research methodology, as the basic foundation for social investigation of linguistic phenomena, evokes the concepts of knowledge and their characterization. By thinking about its path from philosophical knowledge, going through the theological, the empirical and later, the scientific, one can analyze how significant for the production of science is the adequate selection of contextualized and relational methodologies to the object of research.

The systematization and the interrelation of the elements that make up the scientific methodology provides proof of its own social nature. In the introduction, when the theme to be developed is presented in a broad way and how it relates to its proper area of knowledge, the problem, objectives and justification are presented. The problem is the authentic situation of difficulty. The capacity to operate with circumscription is not observed in language, since its interdisciplinary nature relates to the cultural elements of the social world.

The objectives refer to the general character, to what is intended to be achieved, and the specifics, as it is intended to be achieved, the possible "paths" for action to be taken. The justification brings the importance, the opportunity and the viability of the project to be executed. The literature review comprises the systematic organization of the reading understood for the production of language research. The credibility of the proposal depends on the theories to be discussed in the development of the work related to its respective theoretical framework and the state of the art.

Thus, this step requires from the writer a broad reading of general knowledge, a specific reading to consolidate the theme and propose comparisons between one line of thought and another and, especially, the updating of knowledge and practices relating to the object, being important the affiliation in a theory that is relevant to the proposed study. The word method comes from the Greek: methodos - meta and hodos - caminho. To use a method for a research is to select possible paths to reach the proposed objectives, in an orderly and regular manner.

The methods are: approach, procedure, research techniques and analysis. The former are subdivided into: deductive, inductive, hypothetical-deductive and dialectical. The procedure methods are systematized into: structuralist, functionalist, statistical, case study, historical, comparative and dialectic. The research techniques establish the necessary tools for data collection, being direct (questionnaires, life history, interviews, tests or systematic and assistematic observations) and indirect (bibliographic, webgraphic and genres of the academic sphere: review, abstract and scientific article.).

The analysis techniques are qualitative (phenomenological) and quantitative (statistical/numeric). The bibliographic review and references are instances of theoretical basis with scientific legitimacy. The first one infers an organizational value, of everything that was read, in order to present what was really used, by means of filings and instruments of reading order. The bibliography comprises references that can be bibliographical, webgraphic, scientific article, abstracts, reviews and other genres from the academic sphere.

The classes of statements refer to the set of elements of academic writing that are systematized into analytical, responding to formal sciences, and synthetic, related to factual sciences. Postmodernity has proved the need for a qualitative leap towards the social sciences, relational in nature, non-deterministic and mediated by the symbolic. The elaboration of the scientific text corresponds, then, to the methodological universe conceived in an objective and subjective way, of explanation, prediction, interpretation and understanding.

All this in an extensive way, corresponding to the nature of the paradigms of science and their elements of production of meaning. The understanding that language as an irruption of the ideological is the basis of social formations has made possible a new form of research in this area. The types of truth used in the production of a scientific work focused on language, contemplating the social orientation of the word, are based on the formal, contingent, factual and social aspect.

The basis of the conceptual and theoretical component and its assertion in the symbolic world through transactional relationship operations ensures that the research subject is unique and spatial situated in variable and multiple objects in the various areas of knowledge. It is in this aspect that there is the understanding of academic writing, being the individual, in this orientation, all those who mobilize themselves in action because they were persuasive.

Thus, thematic alignment is possible through these types of truth and by the orientation of the author, which is plural. The acceptable paradigm for the natural sciences is of an explanatory nature. Their followers are called methodological monists, and for them there is only one research model for the natural and social sciences. In contrast, the methodological dualists argue for two methods, one for the natural sciences, explanation and prediction, and the other for the social sciences, which is interpretation and understanding.

It is fundamental to conceive that society is not explained, but understood, because the subject is situated historically in a social and ideological context. In the onomasiological orientation, the symbolically mediated subject is the producer of a type of text that contemplates his eminently subjective nature. The weakening of objectivity as an undeniable assumption of science was conceived from the assertiveness of value-mediated research, since there was thus a break with the superficiality of deterministic rationalism.

In an instance of complexity that institutes the dynamic interrelations between the actors and historical-social co-authors, it is not inferred that thinking is based solely on reason and impregnated with limitations and stigmas of absolute social classes and categories. This assertiveness is only possible in the course of the paradigm, because between the borders and limits of any human activity the identities of the subjects who produce science are organized and reorganized. The scientific paradigm accommodates the way of thinking of the subject who selects it.

The four paradigms of science that are presented to be accepted as paradigms of scientific research are, respectively, Positivism, Postpositivism, Critical Theory and related ideological postures and Constructivism. The ontology, epistemology and methodology are constituted in the composition of this framework that conducts the research process. In this case, it is worth highlighting the subjectivity of the nature of language as a factor of materiality and subject heterogeneity.

Thus, the reflection on conceptions of reality, its relationships and characteristics is presented. The ontology deals with the definition of being and demarcates the fundamental categories of it, taking as its parameter its property, system and structure of basic constitution. The Epistemology or theory of knowledge is the aspect of philosophy that deals with philosophical problems related to belief and knowledge. From Plato there is a clear and explicit opposition between belief, in the sense of opinion, and knowledge. In this perspective, belief is analysed as a subjective presupposition in the counterpoint of knowledge, which is the true and justified belief.

Plato's theory deals with the description, explanation and prediction of what is real, what happens, why it happens and how it is based on it, and, through this knowledge, has the pretension of anticipating reality. The criteria of truth recognition are also the object of study of epistemology. In this course, the evidence does not occur as a mere feeling of the truth of thought, but as the full proof.

It is important to relate this idea to the conception of cognition, which is a very ancient word and has its origin in the writings of Plato and Aristotle and can currently be defined as "the act or process of knowing, which involves attention, perception, memory, reasoning, judgment, imagination, thought and language". (FERREIRA, 2009). It is important to emphasize that for the Discourse Analysis there is no clarity or evidence, because the relations of senses are moving and cognition gives space to the constitution of senses proper to language.

As far as the epistemological universe is concerned, positivism is presented in a dualistic/objectivist way, refuting scepticism and ratifying the fact through true conclusions. Positivism is based on a modified dualism/objectivist in an objective manner. There is in this model the possibility of falsifying the discoveries, even though they are probably considered as true.

In critical theory, a transactional/subjectivist posture is observed, and in constructivism, a transactional/subjectivist posture is observed, so that the results or discoveries are constructed, that is, the data does not exist in the empirical world, it is a creation of the researcher, based on the mediation of the historical and social. The positivist paradigm, in an ontological dimension, is based on a naïve realism of reality, even if apprehensible, with inductive methodology and objective explanation, because being monistic, they defend a single method for the natural and social sciences.

The observation preceding the theory starts from the particular reasoning to the general one. This Cartesian thought does not contemplate the multifaceted, plural and interrelational nature of language and distances itself from the proposal to study it through subjectivity and the subject questioned by ideology. Postpositivism or Neopositivism has as its methodology of investigative work the hypothetical-deductive model.

This fact is based on the identification of a problem, the elaboration of the conjecture, the empirical contrast and the conclusions. In this paradigm, scientific knowledge begins with the discovery of a problem, something that science still cannot solve. In an ontological aspect, the researcher is situated in a critical realism, the real, but apprehensible, yet imperfect and probabilistic. Propositions about reality must be submitted to the widest possible criticism for the apprehension of reality as much as it is credible.

The paradigm of critical theory and related ideological postures is projected to the study of historical realism, in a virtual reality formed by social, political, cultural, economic, ethnic and gender values, crystallized over time, being continuously reproduced through the *status quo*. This reality can be apprehended and shares a dualistic methodological thinking, because it ratifies the need to use different methods for the natural and social sciences. The methodological contribution is based on the deductive approach, which starts from the general to the particular, with the objective of interpreting the facts.

Constructivism is maintained as a paradigm of postmodern science, through the understanding of a relative reality constructed in a local and specific way, being markedly individualized by elements inherent to the symbolic world. In the meantime, reality is analyzed in non-established and multiform movement, constituting something plastic, complex and articulated. Being of phenomenological nature, it is dialectic in the measure that the phenomenon is in movement and will be analyzed from the perspective of its relations.

The realization of language in the discursive event is an example of this dynamic and plurivalent phenomenon. As for methodology, positivism uses experimental/manipulative, through the verification of hypotheses and quantitative methods. Positivism also makes use of a modified experimental/manipulative methodology, since there is integration between qualitative and quantitative techniques, with the insertion of emic points of view.

In critical theory, the dialectic/dialectic methodology for the transformation of conceptions is observed and constructivism uses hermeneutics/dialectics, with Discourse Analysis conceiving Hegel's dialectics in idealism and Marx and Engels' in historical materialism. The diachronic study of Language has presented determinant results for the analysis of the linguistic framework of the immanent system of Language, an analysis that is referred, in Brazil, to the works of Mattoso Câmara Jr.

This study, *in and of itself*, makes the analysis of exteriority impossible, implying the erasure of the subject and history. By analyzing language, in its sense as a function of time, the study of historiography can be understood in an idealized identity form.

Later, it was realized that the Sausurian dichotomy of synchronicity and diachrony would only be the beginning for the displacement of much deeper analyses of language understanding, subject and subjectivity, by overcoming the rationalist and empirical paradigm of language as a system. In the Cartesian view, language as a structure has come to be analyzed in itself, taking as a parameter the studies of modernity.

At the center of these studies was Ferdinand de Saussure, a genebrine who instituted scientificity after centuries of speculative Philosophical Grammar, Universal Grammar, Reasoned or Port Royal, with a linear hue, and Historical Grammar, with Hindu as the fulcrum of analysis and comparison parameter. These studies preceded Saussian linguistics and did not attribute to language studies a scientific state. It was from Saussian principles that linguistics conceived its linear and orderly path, enabling a scientific category to language studies through dichotomies: synchrony and diachrony, linearity and arbitrariness, paradigmatic and syntagmatic axes and acoustic image and concept.

Ferdinand de Saussure also had his literary moments, reflecting the studies of anagrams, but his greatest contribution is in the institution of science at a time when language studies lacked regularity. Saussian linguistics is structuralist in nature, and its followers have attributed the name structure to what was named a system. The 1916 Course in General Linguistics, a work compiled by Bally and Sechehaye (CLG, 1916), brings the Sausurian presuppositions and their principles and dichotomies, which would become the foundation of modern linguistics. The Language Circles of Moscow, Prague, Vienna and Copenhagen, with Troubtzkoy, Hyelmslev and Yakobson, were responsible for relevant discussions about language and linguistic theories, especially in what is inherent to functionalism and the detachment from literary, ambiguous and dual meaning of language studies. By instituting scientificity to linguistics, Saussure started language studies from a social perspective, but about the empirical world.

The studies that took place after Saussure resulted in theories called structuralism, with Edward Sapir, distributionalism, with Leonard Bloomfield, functionalism, with Roman Jakobson, generativism, Noan Chomsky, pragmatic, Ludwig Wittgenstein, speech act theory, John Austim & J. Searle, textual linguistics, Halliday and Hasan, sociolinguistics, Willian Labov, semantics, Michel Bréal and discourse analysis, M. Pêcheux, M. Foucault, L. Althusser, E. Benveniste and M. Bakhtin.

The overcoming of a reductionist idea, eminently textual, comes from the studies of semantics by the Frenchman Michel Bréal, thus consolidating the importance of meaning for post-modern studies in the country. Desttut de Tracy, in defining ideology as observation of man in interaction with the environment, impregnated the term with a positive idea, being Bonaparte and Marx and Engels responsible for the inversion of this logic.

But it was with Louis Althusser and the institution of the Ideological Devices and State Repressors, Paul Ricoeur, with the idea that ideology is operative and not thematic, acting in us and for us, Foucault, with his definition of discourse as dispersion, without any principle of unity, and Michel Pêcheux, who conceptualized discourse as a determined form of historical and linguistic materiality, interconnected with ideological materiality, that Discourse Analysis occupied its status as postmodern critical theory of the relationship between subject and exteriority. By conceiving of the subject as a "place of historically constituted significance" (Orlandi, 1996) and of language as a social practice in which exteriority is constitutive, discourse is defined by the determination of language in relation to history.

The theoretical object that is the discourse complains about ideology and historicity. In this perspective, we perceive a propitious moment for the theoretical reorganization of language studies and from it to understand how the production of senses takes place, because, in discourse, more than acts:

"we mean ourselves and thus mean the world itself" (Orlandi, 2012).

The language is not transparent and there is no evidence or pre-existing meaning, because it is built on its historical determination. It is in the reflection produced between subject and sense that multiple meanings are produced. And, thus, by signifying the world, its social reality and its surroundings, it also signifies itself. In this orientation, thought is only valid for action.

And action always has to be mediated by thought. This pragmatic orientation understands that the ideological processes of assujeitamento and masking of reality must be understood in an inter-relational way between man, exteriority and historicity. The symbolic act of constituting meanings implies the offering of a critical theory that is responsible for the constitutive action of the subject towards society, through discourse as linguistic and historical materiality. To have a theory, then, is to offer an effective consubstantial basis of relative constitutive freedom capable of social transformation.

In this way, the state of the art becomes an instrument for action. According to Lorenz and Popper (1990), "The future is open" and this is the nodal point of the issue involving the social reach of science in the most distinct fields of knowledge. Research implies participating in a social reality in direct relation between language and the world. When an interpretation is based on this ideological constitution, it is possible to think about the taxia of the issue that involves the weakening of the conception of language as a communication instrument capable of transmitting information.

Language as a code restricts reading and does not extrapolate the notion of verbal communication elements. It is not enough to read as a naive relationship, or even if it is a naturalization of reading techniques and gestures. It is necessary to read outside the tautological sense, providing a web of meanings. When we think about it, we cannot dissociate this question from the trivialization of art, which is an indispensable component of any curricular matrix that proposes reading in the orientation of discourse, as "a displacement in the network of affiliations of the senses" (Pêcheux, 1992).

Art, in this proposal, is breaking the present condition of any situation, because it removes self-knowledge, what I really am and starts to claim senses. Then, this form of valuation of reality ceases to have an instrumental character and starts to delineate the social boundaries capable of organizing and reorganizing identities. This is only possible if rationalist thought and the deconstruction of what is understood as logic; the conversational, philosophical and mathematical.

The reason is not the instrument responsible for the constitution of language, because ideology is inscribed in the social reality mediated by the subject and the symbolic. The resources of discourse are different from rational logic, which is driven by determinism and linearity. And this crystallized way of conceiving the inertia of things as a fact is that it structures thought along a homogeneous and reductionist line of perceiving the social and reproducing without acting on it.

The comparison and even the replacement of pre-established models by modern science is no longer effective in contemplating the complexity of social interactions. Metonymy is invalid in this case, because the equivalence between the part and the whole is not configured in the restricted and conclusive manner imagined by the Cartesians. It is necessary to detach from representation, displacement and condensation, as associative chains for dialectic interpellation, of the imaginary, exteriority and historicity.

The answer could be in Merleau Ponty, who was a partisan philosopher of phenomenology and thus started from the assumption that speech is an unfolding of the body and the body is an unfolding of the world; he considers reading a unique experience, which articulates the author's speech and the reader's speech. For Merleau-Ponty (2002, p. 35, 36):

"This spot of light that marks two different points on my two retinas, I see it as a single spot in the distance because I have a look and an active body, which take in front of the external messages the convenient attitude so that the show is organized, scalable and balanced". (Merleau-Ponty, 2002, p. 35, 36).

PSYCHOPATHOLOGIES

Psychoanalysis as a theoretical, methodological and practical triad has in its essence the studies of the unconscious and of a cleaved, split and cut subject. Also, in the schools of thought, that is, in the seven schools of psychoanalysis, one finds the object updated by the psychoanalytic lens in transversalization with the cultural matrix of the binary time-space relationship. This tripartition brings other horizons of expectations: Freudian metapsychology, psychic instances, evolution of the cut in the constitution of psychoanalysis and the proportionality of the object as a structure for a possible diagnostic approach.

The transdisciplinary space brings an inseparable condition of dialogic thinking and a dynamic object that is factual, in the diffuse inconstancy of temporality. The unconscious is related to facts that are possible to instar in the memory, and this memorable signification adjusts to the possibilities of the cognizant subject. In the undoubted relationship between the cortical surface and its reactions by the hippocampus, this subject erupts in the reactions produced by his constant activities of emitting data to the cortex, which, even in the stage of sleep (rem), in a *non-contact-responding* character, has in this bijetora function, the registers of information processing, in the silent *delta wave*, thus potentiating the action traversed in the axon of the neuron. There is no doubt that

"the brain is supplied by the eyes, ears and other senses, and the unconscious translates everything into images and words." (HASSIN, 2005).

Would a supposed amalgamation between the disparate fields of mind and brain be methodologically feasible, given the fundamentals of the paradigm of science? It's unlikely. Voices from two domains so epistemologically and methodologically founded on a transcribed and observable confluence inscribed in subjectivity have not reverberated. The correlations are unquestionable, yet a deeper analysis points a totally parallel course.

The new image of unconscious processes initiated in the past decade brings a movement of new possibilities between unconscious processes and their relations with prescribed and clamped activities as being the prerogative of complex brain processing of conscious resources and processes, both with respect to behavior (observable and measurable actions) and complex processing of information or search and self-regulation.

The way to analyze and present studies on the functioning and processing of brain and mind information, in a biunivocal systematic way or in a parallel way is quite different from the last century. It is recognized, then, that the psychoanalytic lens updated its interface relations and, possibly, the neurosciences concatenated part of semantic and historical fragments that made its updating in this field impossible.

In the current view of the neurosciences on the functioning of the brain-mind system, most mental activity is unconscious and only a small part is involved in conscious mental processes (Damasio, 1999, 2000, 2003; Squire & Kandel, 2003; Schacter, 2003; Squire, 1987).

The book entitled *The New Unconscious (Hassin, Uleman & Bargh, 2005)* re-reads the notional proposition of the unconscious under the lens of the social and the neuroscientific and also ratifies the possibility of the unconscious processes being involved in the complex processing of information in fields that differ from the subject's expectations, as well as in the elaboration of projects and attainment of goals and objectives proposed, being seen, a posteriori, as cortical functions of cognitive components.

(...) it is about doing the theory of science, the theory of the subject producing science, that is, doing the theory of the psychism. How do the two coexist and coexist and what does that mean? "(Green, 1995: 30)

Green's analysis of the impossibility of making science out of the science-producing subject is like raising the concept of transference in Psychoanalysis, which appears in its psychoanalytic specificity, as displacement by a lens possibly updated by the discontinuous space-time cultural matrix.

"(...) a process by which unconscious desires are updated on certain objects within the framework of a certain type of relationship established with them and, eminently, the framework of the analytical relationship. This is a repetition of childish prototypes, lived with a strong sense of actuality". (Laplanche and Pontalis, 1994: 668).

The evaluation that relates the memory in a contextualized way is elaborated by the cerebral structure of complex order, called hippocampus, which can be systematized in head, body and tail. This important brain structure is located at the base of the temporal lobe, thus resting on the para-hypocampal gyrus. It is also of functional responsibility of this machinery the reactions of fear inherent to the representations of the subject's stressful experiences, of the imagetic and social relations that are integrated and reintegrated into the memory in a different and dynamic way.

The psychoanalytical method differs from the methods of traditional science in that it does not dispose of the principles of fallibility, popperian fallibility or refutability of the philosopher Karl Popper. The thought of this famous Austrian had its movement in the creation of a group of scientists in the last years of the 1920s, with the objective of an intellectual project, with scientific rigor (language and logical procedures). The falsehood is the assumption of the possibility of a theory being false, which denotes its scientific proof. It is, then, in the doubt that consists the ethereal essence of scientific nature. In Popper's philosophical orientation, the tripartite problem, conjectures and falsification consolidate the three moments for the achievement of a research, in another way, the conflict, the experiential proof and the confirmation that a certain theory or postulate can be false. Psychoanalysis, therefore, does not have this economic nature and would not be subjugated to pass through Ockham's razor, or the principle of parsimony, not even Popper's philosophy of critical rationalism, which has progressiveness as its foundation and not accumulative and inductive knowledge.

In view of what had been presented as a scenario of research and science parallel to the proposals of scientifically proven, cumulative and irrefutable knowledge, psychopathology appears as

branch of science that deals with the essential nature of mental illness, its causes, the structural and functional changes associated with it and its forms of manifestation (Delgalarrondo apud Campbell, 2000).

On the other hand, Karl Jaspers sees psychopathology as an autonomous science of psychology and psychiatry studies. The psychoanalyst Pierre Fédida proposes a point of articulation between the different areas, according to an epistemic convergence that is the treatment in psychic suffering.

TYPES OF PSYCHOPATHOLOGY

Sorting in the psychopathological field is essential to use the elements that would function as data summaries. The first key is composed of descriptive psychopathology, its object being the form of the symptom, establishing the description of psychic alterations. The content of these alterations is the focus of dynamic psychopathology, the stressful experiences and their expressions. They are the affections, fears, disillusionment of people in their specificity, this is not always possible to be described or systematized.

The second key is a pole called medical psychopathology, thus relating the studies linked to the assertive of brain malfunctioning. This orientation sees a dysfunction, that is, bad regulation in the organ or system. On the other hand, existential psychopathology sees the singularity, the specificity and the unique way of analysing being and understanding the particular nuances of being, in the elementary dimension the historical questions of a symbolic field with meanings and resignifications are based. It can be said, then, that being is the conjunction of all the singularly elementary experiences of a subject who acts in his history and dynamically intervenes in the formations and transformations of his psychic reality.

In key three, the opposition between the objects of analysis of behavioral and psychoanalytical psychopathology highlights a consideration of man as a set of possible observable and measurable behaviors to be regulated. This cognitive aspect is possibly verified and modelable, being of order and conscious formation. Psychoanalytical psychopathology presents a determination of the subject through conflicts and unconscious desires. It sees man as a desiring being always clinging to the symbolic order. It is in the psychism that affections dominate and from the expressions of conflicts, inherent basically in the traumatic content of infantile life, emerge as somatological symptoms.

The fourth key is the one containing the operational-pragmatic psychopathology that is involved in the function of serving as a systematic scope for the constitution of the Diagnostic and Statistical Manual of Mental Disorders-DSM 5 and other manuals, ICD - International Statistical Classification of Diseases and Problems Related to Health and CIF - International Classification of Functionality, Disability and Health. In contrast, fundamental psychopathology refers to the foundation of each psychopathological definition. It is the French psychoanalyst Pierre Fédida who proposes an idea of the significance of the symptom as passion and suffering. It is the *pathos!* The intrinsic relationship of the unsustainable lightness of being involved in a link of passion and passivity before the motility of human relationships.

Key number five is the dimensional psychopathology that predicts the gradual evolution of signs, symptoms and disorders. An example of this analysis would be the autistic spectrum, which analyzes as rain guard and the evolution relations of signs and symptoms. With characteristic, sometimes, comorbid. This orientation is more adequate for an updated clinical context of transdisciplinary clinical work. The segmentation and structuring and analysis of mental disorders in an individualized manner as a nosological entity is the hallmark of categorical psychopathology. This type of psychopathology requires a unitary diagnostic identification and belongs to a biologically demarcated field.

The sixth and last key belongs to two distinct types of psychopathology: sociocultural and biological. The first analyses and treats the symptom as socially and culturally constituted, both symbolic and historical. It is in the cultural matrix that all the elements that will guide to what is normal and what is pathological are based, which would then be socially accepted by a certain community. The focus on the neurophysiology of mental disorder is the work of biological psychopathology, that is, cerebral and neurochemical aspects. The basis would then be the alteration of neural functioning and brain constitution mechanisms.

PSYCHOPATHOLOGICAL EVALUATION: CRITERIA

Psychopathology: foundations and mental functions

1.   The study of the systems: anatomy/physiology/psychopathology, precedes the characterization of the disorders - DSM V - CID 10 - CIF.

2.   Diagnostics - Psychopathological and Psychiatric.

3.   Normality criteria: normal and pathological.

4.   Consciousness: mental functions - subjective and ECG - quantitative and qualitative changes.

5.   Attention: mental functions - voluntary - spontaneous - tenacity - vigilance - changes: hypoprosexia/prosexia, hyperprosexia, distraction and distraction.

6.   Disorders: mania, depression, schizophrenia and ADHD.

7.   Orientation: to situate oneself and the environment: autopsychic and allopsychic.

8.   The psychopathological diagnosis is based on the patient's signs and symptoms.

9.   Psychopathological Diagnosis: before Psychiatric - summary of data/reading of mental functions.

10.   Psychiatric Diagnosis: based on mental disorder - diagnostic criteria of major depressive episode - DSM V - depressed/hipothymic mood.

11.   *"THERE ARE NO PATHOGNOMONIC SIGNS OR SYMPTOMS IN PSYCHIATRY." E. Kraepelin.*

12.   Concept of normality: absence of disease - fulfils diagnostic criteria; ideal - socially accepted - imposed behavior - context - statistics - common - not healthy - hypomania x mania x functional hypermania - family - work - social process - neuropsychomotor development/senility.

13.   Subjective - the patient presents as anxious - insight of illness - persecutory delirium; inability to recognize the symptoms is part of a disorder by itself is already part of it; freedom: psychomotricity and obsessive thinking; operational: criteria of normality imposed before. It is necessary to analyze the whole.

14.   Mental functions; consciousness: level of consciousness; psychopathology: contact with reality; perception and recognition - ECG - Glasgow coma scale; normal

changes: normal sleep and sleep; pathological changes: quantitative and qualitative; quantitative: lowering of the level of consciousness; 1. alert - vigilance (normal concentration) 2. obnubilation - lowering, but with weak stimulus, there is a response; 3. stupor: strong or painful stimulus is needed: babbling incomprehensible words. 4. coma: regardless of stimuli, there will be no contact. Associated syndromes: delirium disorientation, floating character, sleep-wake cycle, alteration in action and impaired thinking.

15.   Qualitative changes; twilight states: alert/preserved consciousness level/the body does normal activities/amnesia; second state: it is as if it is twilight/automatic activities that are not related to its reality; dissociation from consciousness: fragmentation of consciousness/alterations: delirium/without normal consciousness. 1. possession: substitution of his identity by another; 2. hypnotic state: has to do with attention/fixing in a memory and memory (hypertension); 3. experience of near death: the so-called light at the end of the tunnel.

16.   Attention; 1. voluntary: the voluntary desire to fix on something (study); 2. spontaneous: the other stimuli stand out over attention; 3. tenacity: fix attention (hypertension - the stimuli do not affect you/hypotenaz - any stimulus affects you); 4. vigilance: ability to change focus (hypervigio/delirium persecutory / schizophrenia).

17.   Alterations; 1. hypoprosexia/aprosexia: overall decrease in attention/inability to concentrate; 2. hyperprosexia: great ability to concentrate/hyperteness/no influence of other stimuli; 3. distraction: looks fixedly and continuously; 4. distraction: cannot maintain fixation/any stimulus calls attention - distracted (dubitative term).

18.   Disorders that can alter attention; 1. mania - hyperpsychism/active/anything calls attention; 2. depression - hypertensiveness; 3. schizophrenia - changes in sense perception - there are more stimuli than others/hypervigious/delirium persecutory; 4. ADHD - attention deficit/incapacity to concentrate.

19.   Orientation - is the ability to situate oneself: who I am/ how many years I have/ perception and knowledge of oneself. 1. autopsychic: *oneself;* 2. allopsychic: environment; 3. vulnerable to brain dysfunction or damage; 4. temporal is more sophisticated than spatial; 5. neuropsychomotor: child orients himself/herself in space first; 6. orientation damage is easier in temporal.

20.   Changes; 1. level of consciousness - decrease / decrease; 2. memory - will not remember; 3. apathy - disinterest; 4. delirious - another reality; 5. dissociation - fragmentation of consciousness. Example: dementia.

PSYCHOANALYTICAL PATHOLOGY

To understand the dynamic nature of the symptom in a psychoanalytic lens of cultural matrix, a historical incursion is necessary, as the constitution of the subject affected by the symbolic, the history, the real of the language. Desttut de Tracy, in defining ideology as the relationship of man with the medium, impregnated the term with a positive idea, and then Bonaparte and Marx and Engels tried to reverse this logic. Althusser, Pêcheux, Foucault and Ricoeur analyzed the discourse under a matrix and catalytic lens, contributing to this tessitura of interconnected elements tinged by the understanding that extrapolates a restricted thought of masking reality. It is impossible to escape from ideology, because it constitutes us; it operates for us and over us.

"Thus considered, ideology is not a concealment, but a function of the necessary relationship between language and the world" (ORLANDI, 1999, p.47).

When talking about Psychoanalysis, such a study is immediately related to Freud, since it is in it that all the precepts referenced by the study of the unconscious are based. According to him, the theories of sexuality and the unconscious mind are the basis of every psychoanalytic study.

In its genesis, the understanding, understanding and applicability of the theory of the human psyche are observed in this universe: its establishing source, form of action and its constitution. Studies on the process of appropriation of knowledge and its application in the social world are closely related to the assumptions of psychoanalytic theory.

Psychoanalysis is thus a theory that has as its principle the understanding that behavior and feelings are governed by unconscious desires, and that mainly cases of neurosis and psychosis are treated by this therapeutic method idealized by S. Freud. In this sense, the unconscious contents of words, actions and imaginary productions of an individual are treated by the psychoanalyst's analysis, based on free associations and transference. It emerges from this that, since it is a clinical and theoretical field of investigation of the human psyche, independent of psychology, it has its origin in medicine, a theory developed by this psychoanalyst.

The theory of Psychoanalysis contributes greatly to the understanding of the constitution of the subject. It is not pertinent, after Freud, to analyze childhood in a restricted way, as a bridge marked by organic development. We are beings affected by the symbolic and through it we become agents of our history, because we are not biologically created but historically formed.

Michel Pêcheux (1938-1983) presents a theory that is based on the conception materialized in ideology and of how ideology manifests itself. The discourse for Pêcheux is the space that derives from the relationship between language and ideology, as an effect of senses. Thus, the explanation of the mechanisms of historical determination of the processes of meaning is the major objective of the discourse analyst and it is by the analysis of the discursive functioning that this is achieved.

It is important to emphasize the influences of Althusser and Canguilhem in the works of Pêcheux, because from the theoretical contributions of these authors, a transformation was proposed in the practice of the human and social sciences, through an analysis about the philosophy of empirical knowledge and the history of epistemology. The question that involves the political and the symbolic is seen as a space for confrontation and it is from this idea of confrontation that questions are first perceived to Linguistics about the excluded exteriority and, in this orientation, also questions the Social Sciences about the transparency of language, the foundation of the evidence to which these Sciences are conceived.

A system subject to ambiguity, this is how Pêcheux considers discursiveness. The deutomatization of language is the fluid nature observed by the autonomy instituted by the relations of metaphor (transference). Literality is no longer the connecting support where words seek meaning. The meaning is always sought in the other, that is, in a symbolic *locus*, founded on movement because it is historical. Pêcheux has its rhizome constituted by Linguistics, Marxism and Psychoanalysis, but it does not conform to their postulates and questions them about language, history and subject. For Lacan, the signifier is expressed through desire. Thus, one can perceive an immediate relation with the unconscious, immediate but constant. We are desiring beings, then, we are signifiers; the constituted speech itself.

In this orientation, the Saussurian theory defines language as a system of signs, while language for Jacques Lacan is conceptualized as a structure that exists prior to the subject's entrance at the moment of his mental development. St. Freud's speech is discussed:

The expression 'speech' should be understood not only as meaning the expression of thought in words, but including the language of gestures and all other methods, such as writing, through which mental activity can be expressed (FREUD, 1974, p. 211).

The primacy of the signifier (acoustic image) over the meaning (concept) is an indispensable precept for the understanding of the basic elements of Psychoanalysis, regarding the object of this science. This theoretical shift is crucial for the conception of a subject in the field of the symbolic, that is, the very confirmation of the idea of the unconscious structured as language.

The unconscious is not a species defined in psychic reality by the circle of what does not have the attribute (or virtue) of consciousness" (LACAN, 1966, p. 830).

The unconscious consists of the repressed materials.

"The unconscious is not to lose one's memory; it is not to remember what one knows (LACAN, 2001, p. 333).

For Lacan (1956), it is in the systemic approaches to structure that unconscious desire is organized through language crossing the symbolic. It is in this field of language that the subject is constituted in the relation with the other. In this orientation, the symbolic is perceived as an action of decentralisation introduced by the notion of the unconscious, of Freudian psychoanalysis.

The symbols envelop the life of man in such a total net that they gather, before he comes into the world, those who will engender him *"by bone and flesh"*; who bring in his birth, with the gifts of the stars, if not with the gifts of the fairies, the design of his destiny; who give the words that will make him faithful or renegade, the law of acts that will follow him even where he is not yet and beyond his own death; and that, through them, his end finds its meaning in the final judgment in which the verb absolves his being or condemns him (LACAN, 1966, p. 279).

For Lacan (1972) the three conceptual categories symbolic, imaginary and real refer to the symbolic which is the space that contemplates language. It is in this interstice that the subject and the law and order, which are called Other, are related. The subject is circumscribed in the instance of the conscious and unconscious. Thus, it can be affirmed that the unconscious has its manifestation in language and this is represented in the psychoanalytic clinic by means of free association, the faulty act, the chistes, the dreams and the symptoms.

Lacan (1998) describes language as symbolic, since it is through it that the system of representations, based on signifiers, determines the subject in its revelation.

It is through this symbolic system that the subject refers to himself by using language (ROUDINESCO; PLON, 1998).

In the notional act of subject, for Lacan, the subject ceases to be, transforming himself into subject of the unconscious. History has a fundamental role in this Interchange.

The Lacanian subject finds existence at a crossroads where a work on the letter and the signifier and a decentralized position of the self in relation to the process of speech intersect. These two (relatively) independent axes indirectly draw a place whose register of functioning is henceforth ensured by the canonical definition according to which the signifier represents the subject to another.

STEPS IN PSYCHOANALYTICAL PSYCHOPATHOLOGY RESEARCH

The evaluation, be it of any nature, is related to the fact of carrying out an analysis in a specific dimension, that is, it can make use of logical-mathematical reasoning, verbal-linguistic orientation, intrapersonal or interpersonal nature, cultural manifestation, manifesto, personality relations and cognitive and intelligence components.

Thus, this analysis can be of values, with quantitative and cutaneous tangency, being by calculations and guided by mathematics in an objective way subsidizing itself of human characteristics or behavior or psychological. What is confirmed is that the concatenation is in the link with the valuation of the value object with determination given by the one who evaluates and makes his analyst lens valid. This analyst systematizes the knowledge related to the steps of valuation, the forms and guidelines of analysis, with a defined scope and a technique of quantitative or qualitative analysis.

Analytical procedures and methods, whether they are behavioural or objective in their historical-constitutive relationship, are circumscribed in the application of analytical instruments and techniques. Then, it can be said that they emerge from the need to understand human behavioral phenomena and in the prediction, interpretation and explanation of these phenomena. There is no disdain for empirical, philosophical and theological knowledge, but it is in observable, validated, reproducible knowledge, which is the scientific, that we cling to any kind of analysis in the field of human evaluation, it takes place in science and by science.

This series of procedures and methods of analysis of what the evaluation is about has in the scientificity its more specific and effective nature and it is in the sessions, in the instruments and techniques of evaluation that the conditions of the methods and techniques of operational applicability of the evaluation instrument are related. It is always important to base the evaluation on an operative contextualization component, because the context in which the evaluation is inserted is fertile soil of assertiveness and guarantee of reliability.

The psychoanalytical constructs to be investigated are derived from instances of psychic studies and their respective approaches, psychoanalytical, behavioral, systemic and others.

The theoretical basis refers to the precise and objective knowledge of the phenomena to be evaluated, investigating in an operational way the psychopathological components of signs, symptoms, disorders and illnesses, knowing that the knowledge of signs and symptoms enables a psychopathological diagnosis of an investigative nature. It is in the reference of the theoretical, technical, methodological and instrumental/scientific process that the whole evaluation process must be based. It is at the time of data collection that the tools and techniques planned for the evaluation are handled.

Upon completion of the evaluation process, decisions and strategies are measured and result in the operationalization of actions and attitudes, as well as the planning of interventions during the evaluation process. This is the basis for the preparation of the report that will be written, according to the specificity of the previous items: multiprofessional or psychological report, statement, certificate, opinion and report, which are types of reports resulting from the evaluation.

THE QUATERNARY STRUCTURE IN PSYCHOANALYTIC PSYCHOPATHOLOGY

Below are possible steps for the elaboration of an analysis in psychoanalytical psychopathology:

1. **Free association/healing process**

2. **Demand/cure process**

3. **Sizing and resizing of the symptom**

4. **Transfer and Contratransfer**

The coding device is capable of measuring these risks and the probability of index and reference of the symptom addressed in the subject. The evaluation of any nature is related to the fact of carrying out an analysis in a specific dimension, that is, it can make use of logical-mathematical reasoning, verbal-linguistic orientation, intrapersonal or interpersonal nature, cultural manifestation, manifesto, personality relations and cognitive and intelligence components.

Thus, this analysis can be of values, with quantitative and cutaneous tangency, being by calculations and guided by mathematics in an objective way subsidizing itself of human characteristics, of behavior or psychoanalytical.

The basis for the purposes of psychoanalytical evaluation guides the overall and specific objectives of the evaluation work, thus adapting the characteristics of the instruments and techniques to the individuals evaluated in the investigation process.

The ten basic steps of the evaluation process refer to the identification of demand, delimitation of psychological and psychoanalytical phenomena, theoretical basis, data collection, analysis, meaning, conclusions, decisions and strategies, preparation of the report and return or devolution. The basis of the premises of the evaluation, and thus the psychoanalytical evaluation, follows this structure above, assuming acuity, efficacy, effectiveness and reliability in the stages and occurrence of the evaluation process.

The identification of the demand is based on the investigation of the actual demand for evaluation, i.e. the claimant, the person, the school, or whoever requests the evaluation. Thus, it is necessary to investigate the subject of the assessment, the data of the person who will go through the process, understanding the reasons that led to the assessment.

The following will be presented for the codification of possible steps for the elaboration of a research regarding clinical care in Psychopathology, according to the Quaternary Structure:

1. Free association/healing process 2. Demand/healing process 3. Dimensioning and re-dimensioning of the symptom 4. Transference and Contra-transference.

When we think of the Free Association as a method used by S. Freud, in order to make the analysis speak what came to his mind, we return, thus, to Freud's beginnings of the substitution of hypnosis as a resource for the treatment of hysteria, in the first studies on this treatise. The free association of ideas is the promising path towards the access to the unconscious, as it was referred in a *regimen*.

The dimensioning and resizing of the symptom is a binary activity, an exercise in the psychoanalytical *setting* that refers to the analyst and analyzing. The analyst dimensions his symptom by means of the senses, by the way in which he dispenses with a series of events at the core of his existence. He has contact with his griefs and dimensions them according to his egóic property of social representation.

The resizing is a summary task of the analyst who perceives the biases and condensations of his fantasy. It is not just any fabrication; it is a ritual of elements, acts and facts that relate in a dynamic and decipherable way, from the point of view of interpretation. Return to the genesis of the object of recalculation. To proceed in a legitimate way to the call of the real.

The desire of the analyst based on his perceptions, comparisons and sublimations are presented in the demand offered to the analyst. In the demand, one finds what is contained in his libidinal request to the analyst. The energy already drained and the product of losses reveal when analyzing a sense crystallized and stuck in the social.

The transference and countertransference are articulated to the materiality of the psychoanalytical *setting*. The possibility of fruition without the intervention of repression in the clinic takes place in a manner elaborated by the analyst and the empathy that results from the commitment to this relationship, the commitment coming from the analyst, which is the countertransference produces the effect of an analytical procedure. The relationships that take place in the psychoanalytic clinic between analyst and analyst, in the process of transference and countertransference.

There is no cure in psychoanalytical treatment, because we are separated, cleaved and incomplete subjects. The process of healing is the understanding of this lack and their commitment to present their experiences, to the new, to the situations of tension that will make them patients in psychic treatment throughout their neurotic existence.

For a research model in Psychoanalysis, taking into account the studies in psychoanalysis and the decentralized, cleaved, split and constituent subject in history and affected by the symbolic, we can present:

A)   Data collection: information will be collected in processing in order to make a qualitative assessment using the deductive method.

B)   Survey and Analysis of Programs and Publications. The theoretical lines suggested by the program content, the bibliographies adopted and the publications produced by the institutions under study will be analyzed in order to verify how the process of meaning is constituted. The theoretical lines will be combined, related and compared.

C)   Research follow-up: based on statistical surveys, a significant sample of interns will be created in the chosen institution, to verify differences in teaching procedures, search for meaning and possible impacts/influences of the theoretical-methodological bases of teaching and learning in conjunction with Psychoanalysis.

D)   Data Analysis: the data from the documental survey and teachers' follow-up will be analysed to make it possible to verify the initial hypotheses. Studies on the strategic models of S. Freud's Caudatory Thinkers.

E)   Evaluation of the results obtained: the results obtained in the final evaluation of this research may serve to broaden our field of reflection and contribute to the improvement of the pedagogical procedures of the clinic of psychoanalytical listening and the understanding of the operationalization of teaching and learning.

In order to draw up a plan that includes psychoanalytical psychopathology studies, one can then proceed:

1. bibliographical survey on the symptom and problem/demand/ache.

2. Criticism and selection of bibliographical references and anamnesis and report

3. Bibliographic material filing (item 1).

4. Elaboration of data collection instruments (item 1).

5. Preparation of data analysis tools (item 1).

6. Sample Selection (items 1 and 2).

7. Data collection (items 1 and 2).

8. Analysis and interpretation of data (items 1 and 2)

9. Study of strategic models, Report and Presentation (items 1 and 2).

THE BRAIN AND THE MIND

The clinic is based on two paths of analysis: one mental and the other cerebral. I begin the discussion about these poles by the brain, which is, according to our line of psychosomatic study, the smallest constitutive part of this novel. Neurons are special cells of the nervous system. They are the cells that communicate through neurotransmitters, making our actions and attitudes viable.

Neurotransmitters are neurochemical substances produced by neurons. When the axon of the presynaptic neuron is excited, the neurotransmitters are released. When released the neurotransmitters move through the synapse to the cell that will be excited or inhibited. When there is a loss, excess or any dysfunction, this imbalance of production amount is the main reference of depression.

Thus, in the constitution of the brain, we have the neurons, which if they do not react as they should, would result from this change the depression. There are several possibilities of undesirable reactions ranging from stressful experiences and traumatic experiences to alcohol and drug abuse, genetic predisposition, melancholy and diseases in the brain, which are difficult to detect.

The context suggests the disease as a traumatic and degrading situation, but it is from the moment the organism has access to the information that physical wear begins.

An example of this is what we call stress, having the possibility of being originated in depression, resulting in several symptoms among them, ulcer and gastritis.

Anhedonia, which is the loss of the ability to feel pleasure, together with avolution and emotional bluntness are characteristics of depression, lack of willingness to do everyday things, lack of appetite, insomnia and discouragement, as well as hypersomnia and increased appetite are symptoms that appear when the depressive process is triggered.

Another symptom of this process is the elaboration of negative thoughts and the symptoms of obsession and compulsion. This combination of symptoms evolved from various disorders has a systemic effect that, because it is diffuse, becomes difficult to control and follow its etiology, making its cause-effect relationship hidden and difficult. Depression brings this kind of path. Stress gives way to or even articulates with anxiety, resulting in panic attacks, palpitations, refluxes, sweating and headache without an apparent clinical basis.

This absence of a specific point, with this characterization in several parts of the body gives space to the intestinal cycle of constipation (intestinal constipation) and frequent bowel movements. There is also a dermal change and weakening of hair and nails in this cycle. As much as there are trends that support one particular form or another of treatment, with psychosomatics being based on an analysis of a single system related to three subsystems: body, mind and social relationships, orientation is a combined form of treatment.

The causes are treated by sessions of psychotherapies that can be psychoanalytical: the seven schools (Freud, Lacan, Bion, Klein, Winnicott, Hartman, Kohut) and the object of psychoanalysis (unconscious), with a view to the traumatic contents experienced in childhood and reminiscences.

We must emphasize the need, in specific cases of intensity and uncontrolled correction of metabolism in neurotransmitters by means of specialized prescription drug therapy.

There are vital needs that keep us going even when we are tired or without a clear expectation of reaching some external object. Unlike what is thought, the demands of life do not come from what we want external, that is, from our material aspirations. This does not cause us melancholy. What demands of us pulse comes from within. The demands of life then come from within and from the vital needs of existence. The path of discharge is related to the principle of pleasure and comes from within the body. For Freud (1915/2004), the demands of life are essentially those coming from within the body and from vital needs.

The source of the pulse is endogenous, we call it the source of the body's interior, for its constancy and its action lies in the failure of the reflex mechanism to deal with the external factors of desire and how this can be modulated with the internal desire. The experiences and vicissitudes of our body are mentally inscribed and the neuroses are responses to the inscriptions and demands of work to maintain balance and pacification. It is on the boundary between the somatic and the psychic that the pulse is installed.

Freud (1915/2004) states that the pulse is the psychic representative of the stimuli that come from inside the body and reach the psyche, as a measure of work demands imposed on the psychic as a consequence of his relationship with the body.

The experience of satisfaction is the starting point to deal with the accumulation of energy from somatic needs and psychic activities. This accumulation must be released and it is from the experience of satisfaction that we propose a possible resource for developing functions that we treat as cognitive: memory, attention, thought, reasoning, problem solving capacity. This experience is in gradual and experiential maturation, it is not acquired abruptly and fully. Its efficacy lies in constancy and occurs from planning, execution, understanding, storage and reproduction, actions that can be modified for an efficient result.

The depression is situated in the neurosis, which is part of the psychic instances constituted by the framework of Freudian metapsychology. Neurosis has as its object recalculation, psychosis, foracclusion and perversion to denial. This presupposition presents the paternal position in the relations presented in Freudian theory. Depression can become a libidinal economy of the new century, in view of the scarce or emptied transference to the external object, that is, the investment is transferred to the ego, in the service of unrealization.

Apathy, anhedonia, and evolution are new forms of perception of an identification that persists in not clenching the thought, distancing the depressive from the demanding human condition of life. This escape from the vicissitudes of daily life makes a mockery of their energies and compromises their libidinal investment in the external object. This defensive attitude provokes paralysis and isolation, not provoking the disposition of excitability and putting in reserve all vital energy that will be inhibited and lost in channelling and egoic investment.

The World Health Organization (WHO) states that by 2020 depression will be the biggest disabling factor, with the greatest impact until diseases that affect the body with sometimes irreversible damage such as diabetes and angina. Fleck (2009) considers depression more harmful than angina, arthritis, asthma and diabetes. This veiled way of paralyzing, lowering and emptying the subject's expectations in this 21st century receives more and more adepts and efforts for digital media and fabulous relationships of human subjectivation.

The treatment and visibility of this disease alternate between nosological and nosographic, as psychotherapy therapy focused on causes and drug therapy that has the function of regulating and correcting the metabolism of neurotransmitters, i.e. carried out according to the symptoms.

DSM V and ICD 10 have a descriptive way of articulating these symptoms to other disorders of the mind, and it is possible to check the somatization or even the evolution of symptoms from one picture to another.

Psychoanalytical thinking refutes the idea of a unique structure and in a crystallized and full form with a verticality in the evolution of the depressive symptom. In the psychic apparatus, one can perceive from the identity of thought to the identity of perception a set of biases and diffusion in the set of signs and symptoms of the depressive process. It is thus known of its internal cause and in these varieties of psychopathological diagnoses, which are fluctuating and intermittent.

The understanding of psychoanalytic theory and the operationalization of all the objects of the seven psychoanalytic schools allow us to affirm that there is no singularity in the depressive process and that this disease is polysymptomatic and distant, zigzagging in dispersed directions. In other words, depression is plural.

Depression is closely related to neurotic conditions, and psychotics remain inflexible and unchanged. The signs and symptoms are *ad infinitum* enveloping the subject by the annulment of desire, which becomes meaningless to do simple things in life from bathing, watching his film or listening to his favorite music and enjoying his favorite food.

Apathy, lack of mood, lack of hunger and lack of fantasy are part of the symptoms. Depressed people are neurotic and depressed neurotics resent living. They only see pain in life and spend their time blaming themselves for not feeling pleasure and for not giving pleasure. This martyrs and corrodes. That's why pain is physical and plurivalent constituting the whole body.

Mourning for Freud (Mourning and Melancholy, FREUD, 1917/2010) is a cause of relative impoverishment of the self and inhibition of the mechanism of topographic balance, which feeds only one of the instances in the topic. Reactions to loss are of an ideal or material nature. On melancholy, we can associate the various biases that are traversed in the phenomenological Freudian description of the mourning process.

In this journey, there is the impoverishment of the self and one has in it the lost object, which when uncharacterized is depersonalized. It is important to confirm that from this point of view, the psychotic structure is very similar to the symptoms of melancholia, even being a very delicate subject and in the discussions several authors do not agree with this position, we started here to use the Freudian line of clinical reasoning of approximation of melancholia with psychosis.

The most complex in the process of mourning and melancholy is to understand that the lost object does not bring pain, but rather pincers the process of mourning for the replacement of this object, without the consciousness of the identity of thought. For Freud, the painful thing is not the loss of the object, but the hard work of mourning and its *hypersensation of* connection to the representation of the lost object. In this case, it is the pain of connection that demands *hyperinvestment and* not the pain of separation, what hurts is not separating but becoming more and more attached.

We have launched the apparent and decisive distinction for the clinic in the elementary concepts between loss and fault. The defense is in a constant narcissistic relationship for overcoming the depressive process and consequent substitution, as the propelling element of the healing process. In the lack, we have what is the propelling motor of the desire for life and in the loss the incursion in the perceptive identity of connection to the lost object. As well as the antidote of loss, there is only the substitutive representation of lack.

LANGUAGE AND PSYCHOPATHOLOGY

Thus, we will begin the analytical study through the development of language, which is based on two fundamental axes of superior cortical function: anatomofunctional structure and verbal stimulation. The distinction lies in the determining nature of biology and the influence of external environment and conditions. It is important for the knowledge and recognition of the neurobiological bases of language to consider it as being processed in different anatomical structures.

The bioelectric studies of brain tissue and the most different imaging techniques allow a more comprehensive study of the neurophysiology of language, because both speech, understanding, reception and nomination can suffer natural or biology-determined losses.

The basic principle presents predominance of the left hemisphere for language development, according to Kandel (2003), the processing of language in about 96% of people is performed in this hemisphere. An important issue that corroborates the clinical study in question proposed by Broca in 1864 is Wada's test, which evaluates qualitatively and quantitatively the laterality and verbal functions, both with respect to language and its memory.

In this clinical examination, the application of an anesthesia in the left cerebral hemisphere usually blocks speech. The associative areas of the cerebral cortex, two cortical areas which do not normally perform their functions, correspond to significant losses in language, a *sine quae non* condition to exclude the motor and sensory primary or secondary areas of location which control language functions.

For a more descriptive understanding, from the nosographic point of view of the disorders, the areas that will be studied will be called the parieto-occipitotemporal associative area and the pre-frontal associative area. The knowledge of these areas allows a more precise intervention in mapping and in complementary practices that could be related to the specificities of these function control plans.

The drill area is in the prefrontal associative area, it is related to the motor cortex for sequentiality planning of movements and it is connected by subcortical fiber bundle to the parieto-occipitotemporal associative area. It has in the area of Broca what we can consider as an indispensable circuit for the formation of the word and is found in the region of the prefrontal cortex.

Then, it can be stated that in the postero-lateral prefrontal cortex and in the pre-motor part the motor patterns are planned so that the individual words are expressed naturally and received effectively. The parieto-occipitotemporal associative area is an area for language comprehension, object naming, primary lecto-language processing and spatial coordinates of the body with respect to analysis.

The understanding of language and naming of objects is fundamental for the linguistic activities of reception, comprehension and speech to be carried out normally. In the temporal lobe, Wernicke's area is located, with a functional purpose of evoking concepts by means of sound processing, which when received and recognized are interpreted as words.

It is in the act of understanding words that the function of Wernicke's area and any injury in this area is based. But it is necessary to consider the relative association between the Wernicke center and the Broca area. The area for naming objects is on the side of the anterior region of the occipital lobe and the posterior region of the temporal lobe.

Vision and hearing are involved in this process, one with regard to learning the names and the other about the physical nature of the object. This realization is a condition without which language cannot be understood. It is important to consider that even with the polarization of the areas of Wernicke and Broca, reading is a consequence of the integration of the two areas, and this dependence would signal the reception of information from the left visual cortex.

Clinical studies have deepened the mechanism of action, reception, production and understanding of language and a biologist cartesianism is not admissible when losses due to brain injuries or even genetics are analyzed. New cortical and subcortical regions in the left hemisphere have been involved in this process, being essential for language acquisition and development.

The language implementation systems (Wernicke and Broca, involving insular cortex and base nuclei, with function of afferent auditory signals analysis, phonic construction and articulatory control). This conceptual system, which has the function of basing the conceptual knowledge, being regions distributed among the associative cortex of superior order. And, finally, the mediating system that acts in an intermediary way and constitutes several regions in the frontal, parietal and temporal association cortex.

Neurons that relate to each other forming a network and are distributed in various regions of the brain are responsible in a specialized way for language processing. It is the hearing aid that is responsible for synchronizing the auditory signals and, by decoding them, transforming them into electrical impulses. These impulses travel through neurons to the auditory area of the cerebral cortex in the temporal lobe.

The recognition of auditory signal patterns, interpretation, formulation of concepts or thoughts, with activation of various groups of nerve cells is a specific function of the Wernicke area. In the lower part of the temporal lobe, the image of what acoustic signal is formed, and the related concepts are stored in the parietal lobe. We consider the opposite process for thought verbalization. An internal verbalization is channeled to the Broca area, in the lower part of the frontal lobe, to be effective in speech production. Both the motor control areas and those responsible for memory are involved in language.

It is important to stress that more than 90% of the population has the left hemisphere as dominant for language processing, but the right hemisphere also participates in this processing. Brain damage results in language (speech) and comprehension disorders that are called aphasia, thus impairing the ability to speak and understand speech. Prosody, resonance, articulation, voice, cadence/pace characterize speech.

When the language changes, we can classify them as: deviation, delay and decoupling.

Language Changes			
Item	Deviation	Delay	Dissociation
1	StandardEvolution	ProgressionLanguage	DistinctionSignifying
2	Changed	Slower pace	Relationship Areas
3	AnomalyAcquisitionLanguage	SequenceCorrect	DifferenceEvolution

Source: Brazilian Association of Psychosomatic Medicine-MT

The factors that contribute to the etiology of learning and language difficulties and disorders are diverse, whether they are emotional, intellectual or cognitive and organic. There are close relationships between certain disorders and language.

CONCLUDING REMARKS

Psychoanalytical psychopathology, by focusing its studies on the conflicts between the unconscious desires of the subject and the result of instinctive and pulsional discharges, sees in the *patho* an action and reaction in what is expected from the vicissitudes of a subject in the face of experiential experiences. In these relationships only desire moves and energises the psychic apparatus. If the blockage in the libidinal investment or the desire becomes scarce, the psychic movement loses its rhythm. To desire something is part of the phenomenon that puts the psychic apparatus to rotate, and in this decrease of pulsional investment, the fuel capable of animating the experiences becomes insufficient and the wheel stops spinning.

According to Freud (1900), only desire is capable of putting the psychic apparatus into action. The primal experience refers to the reminiscences of the baby's experiences that still persist in our body carved in the psychic memory. The prototypes are the hunger and the breast and the search is for the satisfaction of this first experience of pleasure. It is in the encounter between need and the other that tension dissipates and pleasure sets in. This other is what makes the role of promoter of this first satisfaction and of realizer of the function of primary care and protection. The tracing or mental facilitation is the repetition of this activity that is satisfied in the whole process of constitution of contemplation of a perceptive identity, which is also hallucinatory.

Freud's treatment is like hallucination, because the insistence on the attainment of perceptual identity allows for an exhaustive investment in the representation of this primal experience, leading to confusion of sense perception, with signs that refer to senses that are not real in what refers to the temporality of the event, but are in the memory of the subject's recalculated discourse. The imagetic trait left by the experience of satisfaction, it temporalizes in the updating of the saying, which is an action, but does not cease to merge in the hallucinatory act.

In the opposite direction of identity of perception, with the hallucinatory path of desire satisfaction, arises the faculty of thought, which by indirect channel of fulfillment of this experience of satisfaction characterizes what is called identity of thought in Psychopathology.

The body will not be satisfied with the image, it desires the material and this movement will not be able to supply this need, resulting in the experience of helplessness. The wear and tear of investment in this image experience that will not be enough to feed the body is unnecessary, but it ruins the investment that would produce the satisfaction of libido.

The subject does not feel the same pleasure, but is satisfied with the corresponding updating of the experience, starting to seek redress in the loss. In this game of conformation, there are no winners. The mnemic mark refers to the reminiscences of this support that is inscribed in the memory as an image in the scope of what will be the real of the impossible. This satisfaction is hallucinatory and will bring failure in the pulsional investment, because it results in a mental confusion and confrontation between desire and need.

References

World Health Organization-WHO. *International Statistical Classification of Diseases and Health Related Problems. CID-l0.* 8. São Paulo: EDUSP, 2000. 119p.

American Psychiatry Association. *Diagnostic and Statistical Manual of Mental disorders - DSM-5.* 5th.ed. Washington: American Psychiatric Association, 2013.

Dalgalarrondo, P Psychopathology and semiology of mental disorders. Porto Alegre, 2000. Editor Artes Médicas do Sul.

FOUCAULT, M. *Microfisica of power.* Rio de Janeiro: Grail, 1979.

_____. *The birth of the clinic.* Rio de Janeiro: Forense, 2001.

_____. *The freaks: course at the Collège de France.* São Paulo: Martins Fontes, 2001

FREUD, S. *Totem and taboo.* Rio de Janeiro: Imago, 1987. v.13.

_____. *The unease in civilization.* São Paulo: Imago, 1992. v.21

_____. *About the psychopathology of everyday life.* Rio de Janeiro: Imago, 1996. v.6.

_____. *Freud's psychoanalytical method.* Rio de Janeiro: Imago, 1996. v.7.

_____. *The dynamics of the transfer.* Rio de Janeiro: Imago, 1996. v.12.

_____. *Remember, repeat and elaborate.* Rio de Janeiro: Imago, 1996. v.12.

_____. *Notes on transference love.* Rio de Janeiro: Imago, 1996. v.12.

_____. *About narcissism: an introduction.* Rio de Janeiro: Imago, 1996. v.14.

_____. *About transitority.* Rio de Janeiro: Imago, 1996. v.14.

_____. *The instincts and their vicissitudes.* Rio de Janeiro: Imago, 1996. v.14.

_____. Grief *and melancholy.* Rio de Janeiro: Imago, 1996. v.14.

_____. *The "stranger."* Rio de Janeiro: Imago, 1996. v.17.

_____. *Group psychology and ego analysis.* Rio de Janeiro: Imago, 1996. v.18.

_____. *The ego and the id.* Rio de Janeiro: Imago, 1996. v.19.

_____. *Neurosis and psychosis*. Rio de Janeiro: Imago, 1996. v.19.

_____. *Inhibitions, symptoms and distress*. Rio de Janeiro: Imago, 1996. v.20.

_____. *The humor*. Rio de Janeiro: Imago, 1996. v.21.

_____. *Beyond the pleasure principle*. Rio de Janeiro: Imago, 1998.

FUKS, M. P. *Malaise in the contemporaneity and resulting pathologies*. Psychoanalysis. Univ. São Paulo, n.9 e 10, p.63-78, jul.-dec. 1998 - jan.-jun. 1999. 174.

GABBARD, Glen O. Psychodynamics. Porto Alegre: Artmed, 1998.

GARCIA-ROZA, L.A. *Freud and the unconscious*. Rio de Janeiro: Jorge Zahar, 1998.

GUARANTEE, J.C.A. *Depression: from symptoms to treatment*. São Paulo: House of the Psychologist, 2000.

HAHNEMANN, Samuel. Organon of the art of healing. São Paulo: Robe, 1996.

HASSOUN, J. *The melancholy cruelty*. Rio de Janeiro: Civilização Brasileira, 2002.

KAMMERER, T. WARTEL, R. *Diagnostic Dialogue. In:* LACAN, J. The Diagnostics Complaint. Rio de Janeiro: Jorge Zahar, 1989, p.27-44.

FOUCAULT, Michel. *The Order of Speech*. 5. ed. São Paulo. Loyola, 1999.

QUINET, Antonio. (org.) *Psychoanalysis and psychiatry: Controversies and convergences*. Rio de Janeiro: Rios Ambiciosos, 2001.

ANNEXES

THE AUTISTIC SPECTRUM DISORDER - THE SPECTRUM

We will deal specifically with Autistic Spectrum Disorder - TEA, however, we can highlight dyslexia, dyslalia, dyscalculia, epilepsy and other aphasia.

The decrease in written or oral language ability resulting from any brain disorder is called aphasia. Disorders of this nature are diverse and there is a multiplicity of tests, evaluations and reports to classify the types and identify forms of intervention, with priority being given to this in the first years of a child's life.

In general, aphasias are systematized into sensory and motor, the latter still receives the denomination of expressive, because it is closely connected to the difficulty in the production of speech, damaging in terms of rhythm, cadence and fluency. Receptive aphasia, or also called sensory aphasia, most of the time refers to impairments and difficulties in understanding speech and language, impairing reading and writing in aphasic patients.

As a constitutive part of aphasia syndrome, we have speech apraxia. In these patients, more than understanding, reading and writing, motor losses are perceived, such as specialized disability in orofacial movements. Since the linguistic nature is what definitely marks aphasia, the inability to develop motor is the disorder that produces inefficiency in the prosodic condition, with gaps, spaces and slow fluency, causing misunderstandings in the joint.

Muscle changes, such as prosody, phonation joint, and resonance, which also involve breathing, are characteristic of the speech disorder called dysarthria. These symptoms have a casuistry in the CNS or Peripheral lesions, with fixation or paralysis in the speech muscles, that is, lack of coordination in muscle control. Even though apraxia and dysarthria are motor disorders of speech, the losses are different at the production level. Fixity/paralysis, lentification, muscle tone are not significant elements in apraxic patients. Ataxia, hypertension or hypotension, restrictive speech muscle movement are specific to dysarthria.

The assessment of the patient's language at various levels of complexity of speech activities, repetition, description, understanding and other constitutive elements of communication and language, in addition to the assessment of the elements that constitute and compete for speech and the movements and tasks involving motor programming.

Studies involving electroencephalographic discharges, seizure attacks, in general, all the symptoms arising from epileptic seizures bring some specific disorders in the current clinical picture of language disorders.

Acute or critical aphasia with transient cognitive dysfunction, Landau-Kleffner Syndrome, or acquired epileptic aphasia, and developmental dysphasia that is clinically related to epilepsy. It is known from clinical grounds that the cause of this aphasia is continuous seizures or activities involving abnormal epileptiform electroencephalography, even if there is often apparent confusion with symptoms of autonomic disorder or auricarticular deficiency.

In the case of dyslexia, it is important to point out that, according to Rutkowski (2003), there is a significant clinical discrepancy when comparing the data of Brazilian children with those of developed countries, with about 40% of them presenting difficulties in writing in the initial years and this percentage decreases to half in more developed countries.

The sensory-perceived, socio-emotional and motor memory are integrities that are articulated for the combination of environmental and biological phenomena in terms of quantity, quality and frequency of stimuli that the environment offers in the learning of language/communication.

The literature is the basis for the analysis of dyslexia, as it is a significant change in children's learning, differentiating itself from acquired and developmental learning. Acquired dyslexia is the result of brain damage in the biological/genetic case. The causes involving the environment or school space would characterise developmental dyslexia.

Neurological, neuroanatomic and neurophysiological factors, those of cognition, genetic basis, premature birth and others as below average weight would characterize developmental dyslexia. Another division of dyslexia refers to the so-called central and peripheral types. In central dyslexia, there is impairment in the conversion from correct spelling to speech.

In peripheral dyslexia, the compromise occurs in the understanding of the reading content, that is, more in visual perception. The phonological, surface and deep types are part as subtypes of central dyslexia, and attentional, pure (literal) or negligent are the peripheral dyslexia. Surface, semantic and phonological dyslexia are more common in so-called developmental dyslexia.

Among the central and peripheral dyslexia, we have as clinical basis the pure or literal dyslexia reading letter by letter preserved and in the neuroanatomic characteristics occipital lesions inferior to the left. The lesions in the left parietal lobe constitute the neuroanatomic characteristics of attentional dyslexia, and there is preservation of the reading of isolated words, but when grouped, the difficulties in reading in the global visual field persist.

The lesion in the middle cerebral artery region of the right hemisphere involving frontal, parietal, frontal and temporal lobes is part of the neuroanatomical characteristics of dyslexia due to negligence, and the losses in reading in the visual field on the contralateral side of the brain lesion constitute the clinical foundations of this learning alteration. The clinical characteristics of deep dyslexia are reading fluency for frequent and concrete words, absence of non-word readings, and blockage in the nonlexical pathway.

Multiple lesions in the left hemisphere and the existence of residual reading abilities in the right hemisphere are neuroanatomical characteristics of this type of dyslexia. Evidence of dysfunction in the left hemisphere middle and upper-posterior temporal region are neuroanatomical features of surface dyslexia, with clinical features of lexical pathway impairment, without orthographic capacity for information.

The last type is phonological dyslexia, which has a clinical basis of incapacity of phonological decoding, damage to the phoneme-grapheme conversion pathway, difficulties in phonological memory tasks, insufficient performance in reading pseudowords. Specific neuroanatomical dysfunctions are not perceived regarding the proper functioning of perilexical processing. Studies that relate dyslexia to genetics consider reading linked to specific chromosomes 6, 1, 2 and 15.

The Human Genome Project lists the DYX1, DYX2, DYX3 and DYX4 dyslexia susceptibility genes. The same specific chromosomes mentioned above have been identified as related to damage in text processing. Changes in written language, be it disortography or dysgraphia, refer respectively to orthographic changes in word spelling, with dysgraphia being changes in letter strokes. The etiology of oral and written language disorders refer to alterations in auditory, cognitive, autistic, environmental or environmental influence deficits, constitutional or isolated delay in expressive language, and other specific language alterations.

The descriptive analysis of these disorders is based, respectively:

1. influences the acquisition of language after 6-9 months, observed changes in vocal quality loss, suppressed consonants and modification of the sound of vowels. Guttural and primitive sounds still persist.

2. The developmental delay in the evolution of language in the child is partially similar to that of the normal child, at a rate of involution.

3. Occurrence of echolalia, inappropriate persistence of the same theme (perseverance), changes in nonverbal communication, stereotypical and repetitive behaviours, restrictive interests and prejudice to sociability.

4. Elements that involve social and emotional risks. 5. damage and delay related to pragmatics and understanding. In the case of other specific language changes, it is a differential diagnosis of exclusion.

The psycho-pedagogical diagnosis of Autistic Spectrum Disorder - TEA, the analysis is based on the explanation and association to the environment, behavior and learning, as a process of systematic articulation of the child's activities. The association has as parameterization the criteria established in the Diagnostic and Statistical Manual of Mental Disorders - DSM 5 (APA, 2013).

The signs and symptoms of Autistic Spectrum Disorder - TEA should appear in the early years of life, compromising both their social, linguistic and motor skills. These abilities are related to your cognitive skills: language, thinking, perception, memory, reasoning. So, because it is a neurobiological disorder that compromises the prefrontal cortex, it is important to emphasize that this area is mature after approximately 25 years of age.

This child's ability to relate to the environment will be severely impaired and it is from this association between environment, human behaviour and learning that the intervention activities will be applied. It is important at this juncture to understand the scope of the spectrum name. There is an umbrella effect in the semantic constitution of this word, reaching by expanding the classification F.84.0 to F.84.9/CID 10 (Artmed, 2013).

The psychodiagnostic criteria present in neurodevelopment disorders (299.00/F84.0) with deficits that are persistent in various contexts present in the media and interaction, with motor damage.

RECIPROCITY SOCIOEMOTIONAL	BEHAVIOUR COMMUNICATIVE	RELATIONSHIP UNDERSTANDING
Abnormal social approach	Damage to non-verbal communication	Deficit of adaptation to social contexts
Damaged social responses	Variation of verbal and nonverbal communication deficit poorly integrated to abnormality	Damage in sharing imaginary jokes
Reduced sharing of interests, emotions or affection	Deficit in understanding facial gestures and expressions	Disinterest in peers and enturmation
Diagnostic criteria A1	A2 diagnostic criteria	A3 diagnostic criteria

Source: Brazilian Association of Psychosomatic Medicine-MT

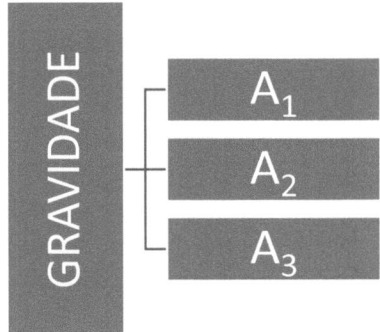

Source: Brazilian Association of Psychosomatic Medicine-MT

The behaviors present restricted and repetitive patterns with rituals in the themes of interest or in the selected activities.

MOVEMENTS MOTORS	INSISTENCE IN MESMICE	INTERESTS FIXES	HIPER OR HYPORREATIVITY
Inappropriate use of objects	Unrelenting adherence to routines	Restricted interests	Sensory stimuli or unusual interest in sensory aspects
Stereotyped or repetitive speech, echolalia and idiosyncratic phrases	Ritualized patterns of verbal behavior	Abnormality and intensity and focus	Apparent indifference to pain/temperature, reaction contrary to sounds or textures
Simple motor stereotype, aligning toys or rotating objects	Strict standards of thought and eating the same food daily	Attachment to unusual objects, circumscribed or persevering interests	Visual fascination by light or movement
Diagnostic criteria B1	Diagnostic criteria B2	Criteria B3 diagnostics	Criteria B4 diagnostics

Source: Brazilian Association of Psychosomatic Medicine-MT

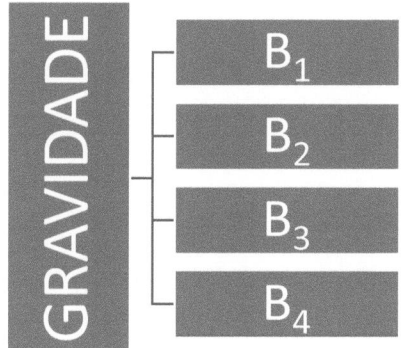

Source: Brazilian Association of Psychosomatic Medicine-MT

The word "spectrum" indicates that when we speak of the autism disorder, we mean that there are different degrees or levels of this disorder for each child. In other words, children diagnosed with autism may present greater or lesser difficulties depending on the degree of the disorder manifested. The DSM-V predicts three levels of impairment (levels 1, 2 and 3). Level 1 is the level of least compromise and Level 3 is the level of most severe signs.

Symptoms present early	Clinically significant damage to social and professional functioning.	Specify: with or without concomitant intellectual impairment, with or without concomitant language impairment, with catatonia.
Diagnostic criteria C	Diagnostic criteria D	Diagnostic criteria E

DIFFERENTIAL PSYCHOPATHOLOGICAL DIAGNOSTIC ANALYSIS - SCHIZOPHRENIA SPECTRUM

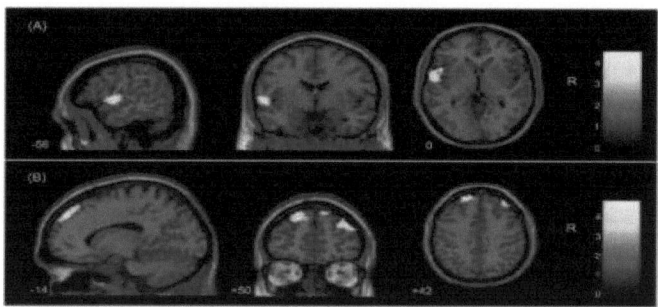

www.napnausp.org.br

The work of differential psychopathological diagnosis is to describe through psychopathology the changes in the new version of DSM-5, which abandons the division into subtypes and the validation of clinical criteria of continuous signs and positive symptomatic periodicity, in the inclusion of prodromic, episodic and residual states, with foundations of the Schizophrenia Schizoafetiva rubric. The symptoms of schizophrenia disorder are characterized by what we call X^2 and X^1, and positivation is validated by X^2, hallucinations, disorganization of thought and behavior, and delusions.

As X^1, we have the negative symptoms, allogy, avolution and emotional bluntness. There are cases of cognitive loss, loss of abstraction capacity, fabulation and symptoms of anxiety and manic-depressive characteristic. The analysis of the *setting* and clinical situation results from the process of *setting up the* case based on the history and cultural aspects and the clinical fundamentals and their absence in differential symptoms of the psychotic disorder.

The spectrum of schizophrenia and other psychotic disorders is a disorder that has a frequency of involvement of 0.3 to 5.7 people per 100,000 inhabitants (MAROT, 2004). This reference demonstrates how significant its study is and how urgent is the expansion of a mental health reception and care network, based on clinical grounds in DSM V - Dictionary of Mental Health - and ICD 10, International Classification of Diseases. Psychiatry is an area of clinical orientation for a systemic reference and effective classification, diagnosis and prognosis for a humanized care with guidance in the promotion of quality of life of the patient and his family.

According to Gama (2004), this disorder affects approximately 20 million people with affective, cognitive and functional losses.

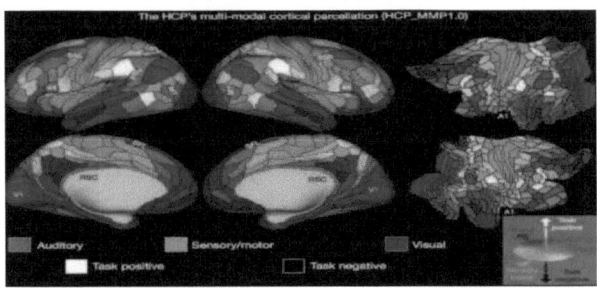

The figure above presents the longitudinal reduction cluster of grey substance, in figure A, with bad evolution and in figure B, with satisfactory clinical evolution. A prominent clinical situation of loss of gray matter in patients with affective psychosis, comorbidity of bipolar disorder symptoms and depression with psychotic symptoms can be seen. In the bilateral frontal dorsolateral cortex the positive clinical evolution shows a marked gain of gray matter.

Changes and Internships			
Item	**Deviation**	**Delay**	**Dissociation**
1	Initial Prodromic	Signs - Initial Symptoms	Distinction Initial symptom significance
2	Acute Episodium	Outbreak accompanied by an episode	Repetition of crises and outbreaks
3	Chronic Residual	Accentuated continuity of negative symptoms (volition, allogy and bluntness)	Accentuated evolution to symptoms of mild depressive disorder.

Author's source

A recent study presented in Nature Magazine (2016) presented a significant result regarding brain mapping in neuroimages dividing the brain into 180 parts, 97 of which had not received reference studies. The brain map relates the parts to consciousness, reasoning, perception, language, sensation and attention functions, cognitive components of importance for both classification and diagnosis and prognosis of neurodevelopment disorders. Disorders such as dementia and schizophrenia may receive considerable clinical contributions by association with cerebral cortex studies.

The epidemiology of the Spectrum Disorder of Schizophrenia and other psychotic disorders refers to the study of this disorder in specific and referenced communities, identifying the risk factors. The heterogeneity and polymorphy in the clinical picture is related to the absence of pathognomic factors.

The lack of occupational or even socioemotional functionality is a marked factor in the positivation of the disorder's symptoms. Emotional and cognitive dysfunctions (attention, memory, learning, language, perception, reasoning, problem solving and thinking) are impaired and are no longer isolated but relational in a network of associative symptoms. The categories can be framed in positive and negative.

Positive are distortions of thoughts marked by delirium and perception, hallucinations, these being sensory, with disorganized speech in relation to language and communication and a disorganized or fixated or catatonic behavior. The negative symptoms are characterized by affective blunting, unproductivity in the logic of thought (allogy) and in the downgrading of the development of social activities (avolition). The falsification of experiences or even deformed perceptions make delusions a mixed content of religiosity, persecution, grandiosity and biological nature.

What is most noticeable are the persecutory delusions, in which the subject in crisis believes he is being spied on or persecuted. Reference delusions are situations in which the person believes to be referenced by comments or gestures and are quite frequent. Bizarre delusions are distinguished from ordinary delusions by a notorious lack of sense and allogy and by being incomprehensible and impossible to fit into the cultural perception of a society in question.

Schneider's first order symptoms are relatively bizarre: extraction, insertion and control. If a bizarre delirium is confirmed, this positive symptom, in itself, is the schizophrenic disorder. Sensory types of hallucinations can be tactile, olfactory, visual, auditory or gustatory. The most common is the auditory accompanied by strange or familiar voices known to be strange to the person's thoughts. Two or more voices talking to each other are part of a content generally characteristic of schizophrenia.

These present symptoms also bring the disorder together positively. Hypnagogic (while sleeping) or hypno-popic hallucinations (time of awakening) are considered normal in the clinical context. The psychopathological aspects must be analyzed so that the level of consciousness and attention and orientation are recognized as cultural and within the concept of normality. Bleuler defends the theory that formal thinking disorder or thought disorganization is a prominent feature of schizophrenia.

The negative symptoms of schizophrenia - development, allogy, emotional bluntness are relevant aspects that take the form of extrapyramidal side effects of the use of neuroleptics, which are drugs also called antichizophrenic, tranquilizers of greater potential or antipsychotics.

They are administered both for mania and delirium (persecution, grandeur, erotomaniac, jealousy, reference) and also for schizophrenia. The competitive blocking of dopamine receptors is an antipsychotic effect of competitive inhibitors called classic neuroleptic drugs.

The negative symptoms and side effects of the use of neuroleptic drugs are of clinical grounds and not of general use or collective knowledge. This statement is observed in the severity of the negative symptoms, thus the severity of symptoms of impaired expression of feeling, disorganized or allogical speech and anhedonia, difficulty in developing social activities, motivation or feeling pleasure. It is also necessary to emphasize the nature and typification of the neuroleptic drug.

When quoting the functional losses of schizophrenia, we can cite personal relationships, education, personal hygiene, work and socioemotional.

Early confirmed symptoms lead to frequent anhedonia accelerated by the symptoms of Mild Anxious Depression Disorder, with diffuse orientation to depersonalization, as an egoic subjective disorder. People who are affected by this evolution of Mild Anxious Depression Disorder present serious risks of suicidal ideation or even of committing suicide.

It has been proven that the vulnerability of a person presenting hallucination, delirium or emotional bluntness, allogy and volition is considerably greater than in people whose symptoms are not in evidence.

This rate is approximately 10% and characterizes a sharp universe of people who already suffer from all the symptoms of this spectrum, because a person who suffers from the schizophrenia spectrum has a family of people who also coexist and administer these symptoms to a lesser or greater degree. This configuration of the relationship between the spectrum of schizophrenia and suicidal ideation or suicide has its predominance in young men.

This family character is the reason for studies and a lot of agreement and disagreement, but the father or mother who has schizophrenia increases the probability of the disease in their children by 10%, with 1% the chance of development in people without this characteristic of inheritance.

Depression and its symptoms are present at all stages of the disease, but there is a way to measure its degree of impact. In the prodrom phase, symptoms occur in 60%, in the episodic or acute period, 75% and in the chronic or residual phase, when it is called "post-psycosis" from 2% to 15%.

These data confirm the coding and familiarity between the spectrum, the depressive symptoms and their co-relationships with suicidal ideation. In these phases, the lack of hope and persistence (resilience), depersonalization and decharacterization of your ego, weakening of your self, guilt and suicidal ideation are perceived.

Anxiety is also a peculiar symptom of the schizophrenic spectrum. Approximately 75% of people in this spectrum use cigarettes or other compounds that have the nicotine. This number is about three times higher than people in general.

As the reaction of smoking is in the action of nicotine on receptors in the brain, there is an attenuation of symptoms and this contributes to the harmful use by the population affected by the disease. It is important to list all these factors that contribute to suicide, because it has been proven that of the people who plan suicide, at least 52% actually try against their own life.

STUDIES ON SCHIZOPHRENIA AND ITS SPECTRA - A STEP IN PSYCHOANALYTIC PSYCHOPATHOLOGY RESEARCH

The study was approved by ABMP-MT, with a Free and Informed Consent Term, TCLE, signed by a family member. Patient C.B.F.S., female, married, 36 years, participated in this study, with initial follow-up in December 2016.

The consolidated diagnosis of schizophrenia was signed by a medical team (Neurologist and Psychiatrist), having as reference the classification and diagnosis, by distance and approximation, by sharing of rubric, and activity of discrimination of clinical entities. As a differential diagnosis of exclusion: depression, brain disease, abstinence, alcoholism and drug addiction (F.10 to F.19 - ICD 10). The C.B.F.S. Clinical Case is based on a transferencial aspect of affective losses from childhood and induction situations, with symptoms of clinical basis shared by the Induced Delusional Disorder (F.24), a situation in which the delusional disorder is shared by two people emotionally connected in an inseparable and unrestricted way.

In this case, only the patient C.B.F.S. presents the symptoms of the authentic psychotic disorder and the husband Z.M.S. induces the delirious ideas. The patient after a frank outbreak and later an episodic outbreak, was medicated with olanzapine. According to Oliveira (2000), olanzapine, a thienobenzodiazepine, is a new antipsychotic that has affinity for D1-D4 binding sites, serotonergics ($5-HT2_{,3,6}$), muscarinics (subtypes 1-5), adrenergics (alpha1)   and histaminergics (H1). In clinical trials, it has been suggested that *olanzapine* decreases the positive and negative symptoms of schizophrenia, and has a low incidence of extrapyramidal effects.

Later, he made use of *clonazepam* and even with drug treatment of this drug, tried suicide 5 times. He is having psychiatric clinical care, with prescription of neuroleptic drugs, because its effects reflect the competitive blocking of dopaminergic receptors, and also anxiolytics and sedatives. The patient C.B.F.S. still maintains the use of neuroleptic drugs, with compensatory effects on clinical follow-up, however there was no evolution of the condition, with suppression of negative symptoms for a significant healing process, with quality of life and effective treatment for the patient. There is no association of alternative therapies or psychotherapies at this time.

TDAH AND PSYCHOANALYTIC PSYCHOPATHOLOGY

Being characterized by a dysfunction in the prefrontal cortex, ADHD has as its symptoms impulsivity, inattention disorders, loss of control of emotions, difficulty in planning, development of strategies and hyperactivity, with hyperkinesia.

According to ARRUDA (2019), 912,000 Brazilian children between 5 and 12 years of age, an estimated 3.3% of the child population, as presented by IBGE. Children with ADHD have seven times greater risk of suffering domestic accidents and nine times greater chance of being hospitalized for bruises and fractures, and in adult life there is also greater risk of difficulty in maintaining personal relationships and greater possibility of developing suicidal ideation.

Although there are indications for the treatment of ADHD using amphetamines and stimulants (Arruda, 2019), it is important to emphasize the role of cognitive components in the "maturation" of the frontal and the significant contribution of psychotherapies and cognitive-behavioral activity.

The diagnosis should take into account several clinical criteria. This clinical condition is very common, so it affects a significant portion of the child population, about 5%, and these symptoms, if not treated, will persist in adult life, manifesting as agitation, impulsiveness and inattention.

The Latin American Research Center for ADHD study, had participation in its research at the Instituto D'Or de Pesquisa e Ensino, in Rio de Janeiro, with representation of Dr. Paulo Mattos. This research included more than 3,000 people, ADHD patients and healthy individuals, between 4 and 63 years of age, who underwent structural neuroimaging tests by magnetic resonance imaging. A posteriori, each region of the brain was evaluated. This protocol can present a comparison of brain structures between individuals with and without the disorder.

The result of the research was very important for the evidence that the structures of ADHD patients such as hippocampus, accumbens nucleus and tonsils are smaller, thus knowing that they are responsible for motivation and regulation of emotions, as well as the so-called reward system. When we realize that in adults these changes are less significant, we have proof that this disorder is related to the delayed maturation of brain regions that regulate emotions and have as audience mainly children.

It is important to point out the difference between Attention Deficit Disorder, of the inattentive type and the hyperactive type, and the impulsive type must also receive specific and directed care. The act of making careless mistakes, difficulty in keeping the attention directive and operative, following instructions, organizing tasks and forgetting, is related to inattention.

The hyperactive and combined type presents the behavior of moving all the time, leaving the place to move around voluntarily, running or climbing, talking excessively, relate to hyperactive symptoms. The symptoms of inattention are most commonly perceived and evidenced in female children. It is important to note that current literature no longer admits a visible distinction between boys and girls when the subject is ADHD.

ADHD is a neurodevelopmental disorder that has current severity specification, according to the Diagnostic and Statistical Manual of Mental Disorders - DSM V, of the *American Psychiatric Association - APA*: 1. Light, with few symptoms, if any, are present beyond those needed to make the diagnosis, criteria met in six (6) months. Other specifications refer to the patient's social, academic or professional life. 2. Moderate, symptoms or functional damage between "mild" and "severe" are present. 3. severe, many symptoms beyond those necessary to make the diagnosis are present, or the symptoms may result in severe impairment.

According to data presented by Sheftall A et al., (2016), ADHD is the most diagnosed neurodevelopmental disorder when studying cases of suicide in children under 12 years of age. Research of this nature points to the need to discuss the importance of disorders that are presented in people who do not yet have their brain regions biologically developed (hypothalamus and amygdala as opposed to the prefrontal cortex). The research done by the American Journal Pediatrics in 17 states between the years 2012 and 2013 brought a significant understanding about the relation of the disorder and deaths by suicide.

The sample was 87 children between 5 and 11 years and 606 pre-adolescents between 12 and 14 years. The procedure was comparative, with one third of each group presenting a type of mental disorder. In the case of children, with a diagnosis of ADHD, hyperactivity or impulsiveness, making up 1/3 and in the case of pre-adolescents, 2/3 with symptoms of depression and dysthymia.

The author of the study, Arielle H. Sheftall, Ph.D., at Nationwide Children's Hospital in Columbus, Ohio, said that in the case of pre-adolescent suicides there was a general pattern of stressful experiences (friends, family, school and affective and social relationships) but those with some kind of mental disorder were more often diagnosed with ADHD.

Other important data relating to this alarming suicide and ADHD situation were presented by The National Resource Center on ADHD (CHADD). BARBARESI (2013) presented results on his ADHD studies based on clinical records of 5,718 adults and found that 8% of the 367 adults who had ADHD in childhood committed suicide, with only 1% of the 4,946 adults without ADHD committing it (Chad.org).

BARKLEY (2008) indicated that adults with ADHD histories are twice as likely to consider or attempt suicide at age 21. A National Comorbidity Replication Survey (NCS-R) study confirmed that of 365 adults with current ADHD, 16% had attempted suicide. According to Agosti (2011), even though the prediction factor for attempted suicide was not confirmed, having one or more disorders increased the risk by 4 to 12 times. (Chad.org)

HINSHAW (2012) after a 10-year prospective study of girls with ADHD in early adulthood found that of 93 girls with combined ADHD, 22 percent attempted suicide compared to the inattentive type, 8 percent, and 6 percent of 88 girls with no history of ADHD. These numbers are relevant to the misconception that the focus on males is exclusive when it comes to identification, diagnosis, intervention and treatment of ADHD.

DISCUSSION

The study was approved by ABMP-MT, with a Free and Informed Consent Term, TCLE, signed by a family member. The research was presented to the Brazilian Association of Psychosomatic Medicine/MT.

This research was done because of the clinical interest about the impossibility of reading and understanding the lecto-writing of the analyzer P.H.B.C., son of K.R.C. and E.B.L., with 10 years of age and attending the 3rd year of elementary school. The picture of this male child is recurrent in learning difficulties, with orientation for neurodevelopmental learning disorders. There was suspicion of ADHD, Attention Deficit Disorder, with Hyperactivity, Impulsivity and Inattention.

The indication from the report of the Teaching Unit is that the analyst did not develop, that he had already "failed" twice, recurrently, and that he did not learn to read, becoming "nervous and anguished" and sometimes stressed and inattentive, when they addressed him. They continued their considerations stating that he "did not listen" and when he listened, he forgot (there was no retention of informational content) what was said. He did not use medication. He did not practice diet or food restriction. He was overweight, based on height/mass matches, and this situation made him uncomfortable, as his colleagues and family always reported him with pejorative nicknames. His first analysis had been made in 2018, however without evolution and follow-up.

Everything begins in the neurobiological control of emotions, impulses, sexuality, instinctive reactions, memory, attention, perception and other components that result from this inhalation, activation of the olfactory system by the olfactory nerves and bulb, providing a directive connection with the Central Nervous System, leading the stimulus to the limbic system. From this process, there is a quotient that reaches the bloodstream dynamized by the respiratory system.

The action of molecules through the skin results in the absorption of therapeutic oils and their conduction through the circulation of blood, reaching the tissues and organs of the human body. The final conduction of therapeutic oils occurs in different tissues of the body, however the passage of these substances from the place of contact is through the intestine.

Lavender is part of the universe of therapeutic oils with a welfare effect, sedative and calming, while rosemary acts on the human body with signs and symptoms of alternation between hyperprosexia and vigilance. In 1988, psychologists from the University of Miami proved through EEG - Electroencephalographic Examination, with 40 patients, the sleepiness effect of lavender, by significant lowering of the frequency of brain waves, in contrast, the alert state would be confirmed by patients with a history of inhalation of rosemary.

The most relevant thing is that by being monitored in tests that required logical-mathematical reasoning, patients who inhaled rosemary essence had more satisfactory results than those who had not received treatment with therapeutic oils.

The brain furrow, called the interhemispheric fissure, separates the human brain, thus presenting two hemispheres. The bundle of neural fibers connects the two hemispheres, left and right, with the exchange of active and complementary information improving the stimuli that apply and operate the antagonist part of the body.

In 2019, other analyses were performed and, through psychotherapies between family and analyzing, the results were successful. The analyzer already shows an evolution in reading, initiating its process of acquisition of initial lecto-written correspondence. Further analysis is needed on the identification of ADHD symptoms, the next step being the reader's constitution activities and, later, the application of SNAP IV, to identify signs and possible symptoms of ADHD, which have not yet been confirmed. The research is still under development. Complementary therapies such as initial aromatherapy and initial chromotherapy were used, together with the initiation of read-write correspondence and activities that are of psycho-pedagogical orientation and correlations with the analysis of behavior applied to reading and writing.

MODERNITY FIRST CLINIC		
1953 – 1970 Lacan's First Clinic	**Analyst Mirroring Criticism**	**Classic Freudism**
1. Paternity	Father/parent guidance	Oedipus Complex
2. Jerarquization	Hierarchy/submission	Superego
3. Intercommunication	Dialogue/face-to-face	Therapeutic alliance
4. Streamlining	Anti-syncretic/reason reasoning	Other
5. Universalization	Established truth / fact	I'm supposed to know
6. Inertization	Static/imobile	Resistance
7. Analyticity	Evaluation/analysis	Hard symptom
8. Training	Attraction/training	Methodology
9 Verticalism	Authority/empty	Specularity
10. Tribulation	Difficulty/adversity	Repression

WORLDWIDE SECOND CLINIC		
1970 – 1981 Second Lacan Clinic	**Analyst Mirroring Criticism**	**Lacanism**
1. Change	Alterity	Collective calculation
2. Dissipation	Reversibility	Radical differences
3. Intradiscourse	Internalization	Articulated Monologues
4. Accessibility	Sharing	Resonate
5. Flexibility	Mobility	Certainty
6. Connectivity	Relational	Interactive
7. Empatibility	Altruism	Responsibility
8. Probability	Vicissitudes	Experiences
9 Horizontalism	Dimensionality	Horizontal order
10. Iteration	Intelligence	Opportunity

THE SCHOOLS OF THOUGHT OF CLASSICAL PSYCHOANALYSIS

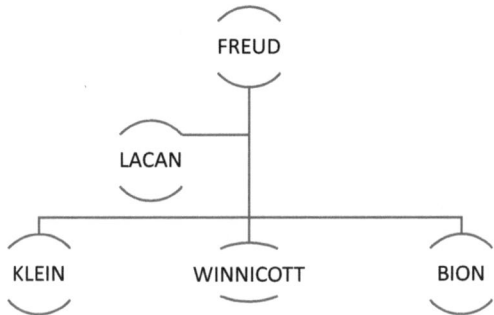

TEORIA DO DUPLO EIXO DE KOHUT (1971)

Ambições

Ideais e valores

Tensão entre talentos e habilidades

Perfeição ao self grandioso (transferência especular)

Imagem parental idealizada
Transferência idealizante

Narcisismo primário (coesão)

Núcleos fragmentados do self

2. Evolução narcisista do desenvolvimento.

Narcisismo secundário (após a rejeição dos objetos)

Amor objetal

Narcisismo primário

1. Evolução clássica do desenvolvimento conduzindo ao amor objetal.

According to Gabbard (1984), familiarity with all three theoretical models of dynamic psychiatry (Schools of Thought of Psychoanalysis: Ego, Self and TRO) requires a greater breadth of knowledge, but also allows a richer understanding of patients and their psychopathology.

It is always more efficient and cautious to use maps, compasses and other cartography and orienteering equipment when you launch yourself to reach a point in the middle of the unknown. The theoretical schools of psychoanalysis are these essential elements, which more than instruments of use and disuse, are mechanisms for understanding the dynamic functioning of the psychic apparatus. They are the safe north guided by the referencing of its objects of study. In the course, at the beginning of this journey, there are at least three in encounter with the imbrication of its purpose: the subject who sees himself (reading of himself), what one sees of this subject (reading of the other) and the subject as he constitutively is (the real of the subject).

DISSOCIAÇÃO DO EGO EM SUBORGANIZAÇÕES INCONSCIENTES DE OGDEN (1983)

Suborganizações de objeto do ego

Suborganizações de self do ego

Internalização das relações objetais

Externalização no terapeuta

Transferência: subdivisão self do ego/objetal do ego

Via de retorno do intrapsíquico para o interpessoal

2. Significados são produzidos, baseado-se em uma identificação de um aspecto do ego com o objeto. A identificação é tão íntima que o senso original de self é quase inteiramente perdido.

Corpo estranho/monitoramento

Superego

Noção Freudiana

1. Aspectos do ego nos quais o indivíduo vivencia mais plenamente suas ideias e sentimentos como próprios

According to Gabbard (1984), the formulations of the objective relationships derived from clinical observations were supported and elaborated by the studies of baby observations conducted by Margaret Mahler. She and her collaborators identified three phases: autistic phase (2 first months of life), symbiosis (between 2 and 6 months) and separation-individuation (four subphases) - differentiation (6 and 10 months), practice (10 and 16 months), rapprochement (16 and 24 months) and consolidation of individuality (third year of life).

Just like magnetic resonance imaging is the most clinician-oriented examination that captures high-resolution images of tissues and organs of the human body/organism, with increasingly modern and practical diagnostic methods, being a powerful and versatile non-invasive examination, nosographic and nosological psychopathology is a fundamental instrument for the investigative monitoring of the entire anatomophysiological apparatus of man. None of this reveals its essence. There is no exam capable of bringing out what is formless. And our subjective nature is shapeless. In order to be the welcome and welcome guest, we must be the messengers of dissociations and, in order to do so, repeatedly assume the imaginative materiality of their resonance.

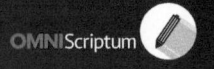

Printed by Books on Demand GmbH, Norderstedt / Germany